What They'r
Exploring Colorado Wineries

"*Exploring Colorado Wineries* is a great resource for those wanting to discover the colorful world of Colorado wine. This approachable guide offers Colorado winery profiles, food and wine pairing suggestions and wine terminology. It is a must have for anyone wanting to expand their knowledge on Colorado's growing wine industry."

– Cassidee Shull, Executive Director, Colorado Association for Viticulture & Enology (CAVE)

"Fortunately for wine-lovers everywhere, Paula Mitchell knows the story and like an alchemist she has turned her knowledge and affection for Colorado's wine industry into a delightful book. Mitchell takes readers on a tour of the people, places and grapes that make Colorado such a fascinating place to make and enjoy wine. Like finding the just-right Reidel glass, this well-researched and engaging book is the perfect accompaniment to a trip through Colorado wine country."

– Dave Buchanan, Wine Writer, *The Daily Sentinel*

"In *Exploring Colorado Wineries,* Paula Mitchell introduces the reader to the joys of wine tasting and touring in the Centennial State while taking out some of the mystery and intimidation sometimes associated with tasting, sampling and enjoying wine. Written simply, this guide has something for the newcomer as well as the more experienced sommelier."

– Jim Clark, CDME, former President & CEO, Fort Collins Convention and Visitors Bureau

"Paula Mitchell's new book is an indispensable guide to exploring America's Wild West Of Wine! It will help you discover Colorado's wine country as well as urban wine tasting destinations. This handy book also includes practical how-to information that is sure to help you increase your pure enjoyment of wine!"

– Christopher J. Davies, Editor and Co-Founder, *Wine Country International®* magazine

"A useful companion for people wanting to visit Colorado wineries, it's especially helpful for those who are just starting in their exploration of the vine and grape."

– Ed Sealover, author of *Mountain Brew: A Guide to Colorado's Breweries*

"You've picked a wonderful book about Colorado wine. Now bring the book and come get a "taste" of the real Wine Country experience."

– Barb Bowman, Division Manager, Grand Junction Visitor and Convention Bureau

"*Exploring Colorado Wineries* is a great resource for wine lovers or those who are just new to the appreciation of wine. This guide will help take you through the wine regions of Colorado with great tips for enjoying this growing culinary industry in Colorado. The book will become your must have companion with maps to wineries, tasting pointers and space to make your own notes as you sip your way along."

– Kelli Hepler, Coordinator, Delta County Tourism Cabinet

"As a lifelong resident of Western Colorado it was my pleasure to review *Exploring Colorado Wineries* by Paula Mitchell. I would hope that the reader gets as much enjoyment and information from it as I did."

– Roger Granat, *Palisade, Colorado*

"Delta County is no longer Colorado's best kept secret. With *Exploring Colorado Wineries*, Paula Mitchell shines the light on our little corner of the state. Use this book as your guide to locating our great boutique wineries. Along the way you can also savor locally grown fruits and vegetables, beautiful works of art and some incredible mountain views!"

– Pat Sunderland, Managing Editor, *Delta County Independent*

"Durango prides itself on being the "City of Brewerly Love" with 6 craft breweries, 2 distilleries and 4 wineries in our quintessential Southwestern Colorado area. The recent culinary attention comes from the increased quality of wines, tasting rooms and wineries in the region. Colorado now challenges some of the finest California vintners. It's refreshing to see a book that gives credit to the quality wineries that call Colorado home."

– Anne Klein, Public Relations, Durango Area Tourism Office

Exploring Colorado Wineries

Revised
& Updated
2nd Edition

Guidebook & Journal

Paula Mitchell

Summit Mesa Publishing

Exploring Colorado Wineries: Guidebook & Journal (Revised & Updated 2nd Edition)
By Paula Mitchell

Disclaimer: All information contained in this book is deemed to be current as of the date of this publication.

Published by

Summit Mesa Publishing

P.O. Box 2134
Littleton, Colorado 80161

Cover and Interior Layout by Nick Zelinger, www.NZGraphics.com

ISBN: 978-0-9851508-2-2

Library of Congress Control Number: 2012932506

Revised & Updated Second Edition 2015

Printed in Korea

Visit www.ExploringColoradoWineries.com (for print or ebook purchases)

To my family –
Jim, Allison and Mackenzie....
Thanks for your constant support, encouragement and reassurances
in all facets of my life's adventures.

Contents

WINE REGIONS

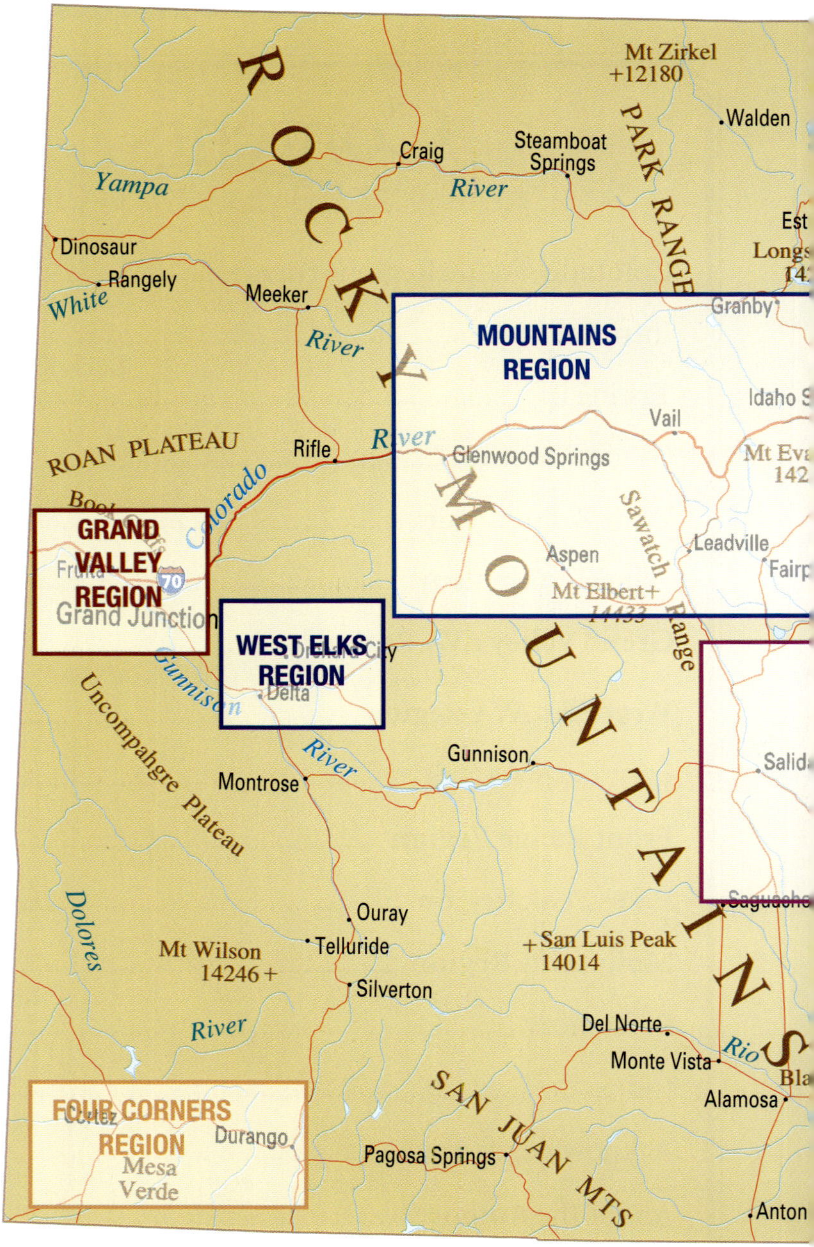

Grand Valley **Delta & Montrose, West Elks** **Four Corners**

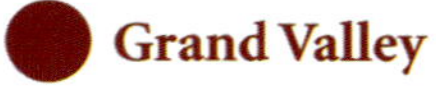

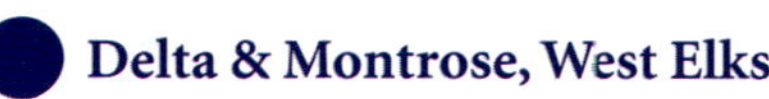

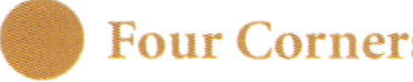

OF COLORADO

Front Range Pikes Peak Mountains

INTRODUCTION

I am excited you want to learn more about wine and Colorado's wine industry! Since the first edition of *Exploring Colorado Wineries* was written in 2012, I've had the pleasure of meeting an incredible group of people—winery owners, winemakers and farmers. In these past three years, I have presented "wine exploring" seminars at a variety of venues to show people the fun and enjoyment of discovering Colorado's wines. I also attended numerous wine festivals and traveled around the state. I even earned my Level 2 Sommelier certification. And the best part, I enjoyed some delicious Colorado wines along the way. It has been an unbelievable experience!

The primary purpose of *Exploring Colorado Wineries* is to assist YOU in discovering all of Colorado's wineries. Whether you are just beginning your wine education, a wine expert or someone in between, I hope this guidebook can help you discover and explore Colorado's wineries and begin to savor their wines!

A Brief History of Colorado Wineries...

Winemakers and farmers have grown grapes and made wine in Colorado since the 1860s. When the Ute Indians were evacuated from the Grand Valley region in the mid-1880s, fruit trees and grapevine stock started to appear. Settlers began making home-fermented wine for personal consumption. Even Governor George Crawford recognized the grape growing potential in this area and planted vines himself! In the late 19th century European immigrants arrived in the area and sought out available wine. It was at this time that both grapevines and fruit trees really began to flourish on the Western Slope.

But then came the Women's Christian Temperance Union and Prohibition. Due to these movements the majority of grapevines were uprooted and replaced with only fruit trees. Although many farmers were permitted to make 40 gallons of "grape juice" for their personal consumption, fruit became the main agricultural product for this area.

It wasn't until the late 1960s that Dr. Gerald and Mary Ivancie along with Jim and Ann Seewald opened a winery in the Grand Valley. Although they sourced their grapes from California, they initiated the present-day Colorado wine movement. In 1978 thirteen people started a winery named Colorado Mountain Vineyards using Colorado-grown grapes, and the current wine industry was off and running!

By the early 1990s many other wineries were beginning to establish themselves. Two American Viticultural Areas (AVA) were designated as well: Grand Valley in 1991 and West Elks in 2001. The majority of the state's grapes are grown in these two areas. Today, the Colorado wine industry continues to expand and develop statewide. *Exploring Colorado Wineries* provides you with valuable information about Colorado's existing winery operations.

How to Use the Book...

The first section of the book provides general wine information, including **Tasting, Grape Varieties, Wine & Food Pairing** and **Wine Terminology**. Increase your abilities through the **Tasting** pages, which review the Five S's of tasting basics, provide wine-related vocabulary and explain how I began my wine studies. Discover the most common grapes grown in Colorado and their typical characteristics in the **Grape Varieties** section. Learn the basic rules about pairing in the **Wine & Food Pairing** segment. Reference the glossary in **Wine Terminology** to help you broaden your wine vocabulary.

Colorado is typically divided into six wine regions: Grand Valley AVA, West Elks AVA area, Four Corners Region, the Front Range, Pikes Peak area and the Mountains. For easy reference I have used that system, color coded each region and included an overall map. The wineries in each region are listed in alphabetical order. Each winery's pages contain contact and tasting room information, the wines produced, a message from the owner and easy-to-follow directions. (Note: Information is accurate as of June, 2015.)

Because I am nearing the age where "if I don't write it down, I won't remember it," I have included a **Journal** section on each winery's page. I highly recommend jotting down a few notes to help remember the wineries and their wines.

Touring wineries with my daughters when they were little was always about compromise (keeping them happy while I enjoyed myself!), so I have included the **What Else To See & Do** sections for each region, listing other interesting places to visit in the area.

Exploring Colorado Wineries is all about reading, tasting, learning, discovering and exploring Colorado's wineries. I hope you enjoy your adventure! And please, remember to drink and drive responsibly.

Explore and Enjoy!

Paula Mitchell

TASTING

To truly know a grape or a wine is to taste it! What could be more fun? Books are helpful and informative, and I highly recommend reading a few on the subject before you start tasting. Nothing, however, surpasses first-hand experience. So how should you begin? Here is how I started.

I first created a "Tasting Journal" (see more information below) so I could take notes and list my impressions about the wines I sampled. This tasting journal can range from a small, simple notebook to an extensive binder full of labels and meticulous details. You can organize yourself in any way that works for you. Just remember that taking notes is important.

When deciding which wines you should try first, I recommend starting with something familiar. For years my wine of choice was Chardonnay, so I bought bottles of Old World and New World Chardonnay and began to taste and compare their characteristics. Once comfortable with the process, I began to branch out and try other common white wines such as Pinot Grigio and Sauvignon Blanc. I would pick a particular grape varietal, learn about that grape and then taste wines from several different regions and/or countries. From my experiences, I discovered that comparing three to five wines at a time worked best. When I gained enough knowledge about a particular grape, I would try another using the same methodology. After learning about several white wines, I applied the process to red wines.

Once you have a basic knowledge of a particular grape's taste profile, it's then fun to sample and compare several different grapes at the same time. An example would be tasting a flight of whites (Chardonnay, Sauvignon Blanc, Pinot Grigio and Riesling) or reds

(Pinot Noir, Syrah, Merlot and Cabernet Sauvignon). You could also increase your proficiency and test your skills by tasting and comparing the same grape from a Colorado winery versus wines from California, Washington and Oregon.

My Personal Tasting Journal Includes...

- Basic information about the wine: varietal, country, region, vineyard, vintage
- Purchase information: when and where I bought the wine, cost
- Color of the wine
- The aromas or bouquet I detected
- Tastes (be as specific as possible)
- Grade (I use a scale of 1-10 or A-F)
- What I liked or didn't like about the wine (be descriptive)
- Date of tasting the wine

Tasting Order...

It is important to taste wine in a particular order. You do not want to drink a red wine before a white, or a sweet wine before a dry, as that can alter your perceived taste of the wine. The standard rules for tasting are:

- Drink white wines before red wines (Chardonnay before a Cabernet)
- Sample delicate wines before strong wines (Pinot Noir before Merlot before Zinfandel)
- Taste dry wines before sweet wines before dessert wines (Sauvignon Blanc before Gewürztraminer before Port)

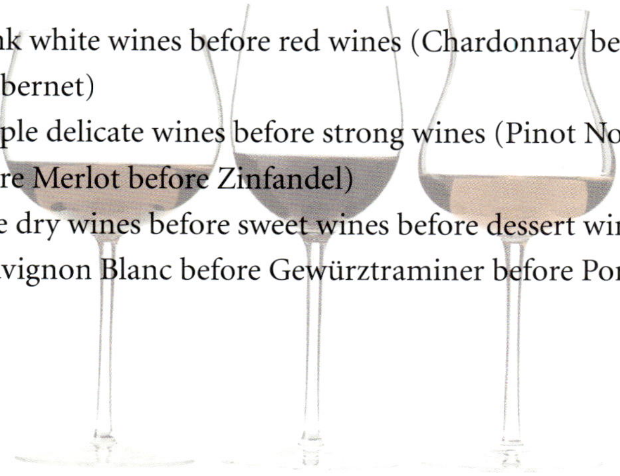

Tasting Procedure: The Five S's...

Once you have your tasting method decided and your trusty notebook in hand, follow the steps below. By following these steps and tasting a few wines, you will become a pro in no time! A piece of advice: only fill the glass with about 1" of wine for tasting. That amount will give you enough to smell, taste and critique without spilling as you swirl.

#1. See: To gauge a wine's color, tip the glass slightly and hold a white sheet of paper or napkin behind the glass. Is this typically the varietal's color pigmentation? The more you try various wines, the more you will notice how the color can differ. White wines can range from almost clear to a deep gold. Red wines can range from a cherry hue to purple to ruby. As white wines age they gain color. This is opposite for reds as they lose their color or brilliance over time.

Traditional Colors in Wine...

Whites:		***Reds:***	
	clear		cherry
	pale yellow		red violet
	yellow green		purple
	straw		ruby
	yellow gold		garnet
	gold		brick red
	amber		red brown

#2. Swirl: Swirling your glass introduces oxygen into the wine, which helps release the aromas or bouquet. Hold the stem of the glass with your thumb and first two fingers and slowly move the glass around in a circular motion two to three times. This is best done while keeping the glass flat on a table! This action brings the wine's fragrances to the surface, allowing your nose to better perceive its various characteristics. After swirling the wine, you may see "legs" or "tears" running down the inside of the glass. This phenomenon is still up for discussion, but know that there is a correlation between alcohol content and legs, not quality and legs.

#3. Smell: Tilt the glass so you can literally stick your nose into the glass and take in a few breaths. Some people are shy about this procedure, so just take two to three simple sniffs. There is no need to take one deep lungful as if it's your last gasping breath! What are some of the first descriptive words that come to mind? Do you smell any fruit, earthy aromas, spices, plants, etc.? The more you taste and experience different wines, the broader your "descriptive" vocabulary will become. Don't be embarrassed if you don't smell anything distinctly, as some wines' aromas are harder to distinguish than others. The Wine Aroma Wheel (see internet) is an excellent tool to help with descriptive vocabulary.

#4. Sip: Take a small sip, enough to fully experience the taste, without being a big gulp. Swish the wine around in your mouth for a few seconds. As you are doing this, what do you taste initially? What words come to mind? What fruits do you taste? Are there floral, herbal or vegetal characteristics? Do you taste the effects from barrel aging, such as vanilla, leather or tar? Next, think how the wine feels in your mouth. Does it seem light-, medium- or full-bodied? (like how water, milk, cream feels in your mouth) Does the wine seem balanced between its fruit / acidity / tannin? Does anything stand out as unpleasant?

#5. Savor: After you swallow the sip, what else comes to mind? Your first question should be "did I like it?" Did your mouth pucker (tannin) or salivate (acidity)? Was there an aftertaste? Were there any other flavors that you didn't experience during the sipping phase (complexity)? What other words could you use to describe the taste?

The most important result from the Five S's tasting procedure is...whether YOU liked it? No matter what other people may taste in the wine or say about it, how much the wine costs, who produced it, etc., the main point is your opinion of the wine. Are you interested in taking another sip, having a whole glass, buying a bottle, or buying the winery? If your reaction was negative, why? These reasons are important when deciding what wines to taste next.

Descriptive Words...

Kevin Zraly, a world-renowned wine author and educator, provides his students with a list of 500+ words to describe wine. Trying to figure out what words to use from that many options can be overwhelming, so here are the top words I commonly use to describe a wine's characteristics.

acidity
aroma
astringent
balanced
barnyard
big
bitter
body
bouquet
buttery
burnt rubber
caramel
chewy
chocolate
citrus
color

complex
crisp
delicate
depth
dry
earthy
finish
firm
floral
fresh
fruity
funky
gamey
grassy
herbal
honey

leather
light
mature
mineral
musty
oaky
nutty
pencil lead
pepper
perfumed
powerful
pungent
rich
short
soft
smoky

spicy
sweet
tannin
tar
tart
thin
toasty
tobacco
vanilla
vegetal
vinegar
which fruits?
woody
yeasty
young
yuck!

Basic Fruit Categories…

- Red fruits: strawberry, raspberry, red current, cherry
- Black fruits: plums, blackcurrants, blackberry, black cherry
- Pome: apple, pear
- Drupe: peach, apricot, mango
- Tropical: pineapple, passion fruits
- Citrus: lemon, grapefruit

How to Read a Wine Label...

Reading an American (Colorado) wine bottle label is fairly simple compared with Old World wine labels. Below is the standard information contained on a label from the United States.

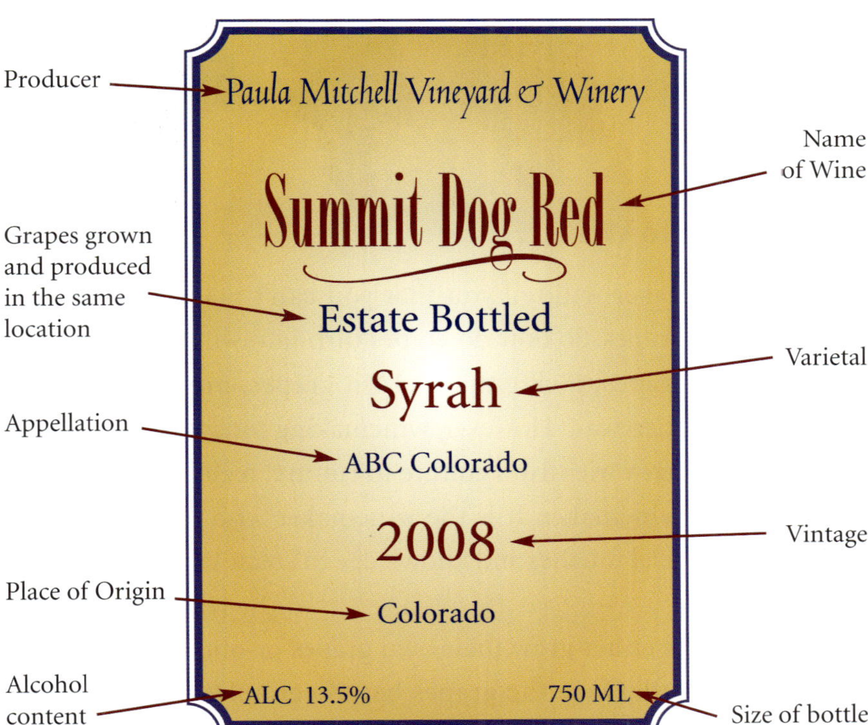

GRAPE VARIETIES

Fun Facts about Grapes...

- *Vitis Vinifera* is the most common species used for winemaking.
- Grapes grow in both the northern and southern hemispheres, between the 30th and 50th parallels.
- There are three major grape growing macroclimates: Maritime, Continental and Mediterranean.
- Grapevines grow best in well-drained and relatively infertile soils like chalk, clay, granite, limestone, sand and schist.
- Grapevines have a yearly cycle, including a dormancy period.
- Some grapevines live for over 100 years, but the prime producing years are from 10 to 30 years old.

From Grape to Wine...

Any winemaker will tell you that you can't make a great wine without great grapes. So how do grapes turn into wine? It can be this simple: grow grapes, pick grapes, crush grapes, put grapes into a container and then wait. However, winemaking today is a complexity of techniques that varies from culture to culture, region to region and winemaker to winemaker. It is the winemaker who ultimately adds his/her own special touches and knowledge to create a wine unlike any other.

Winemakers either grow their own grapes or obtain grapes from another vineyard. Once the grapes have been selected and picked (timing and the percentage of brix (sugar) in the grapes is critical), they are crushed. This is usually accomplished by a programmable machine known as a crusher-destemmer. Just after crush begins the slight variation in how red wines and white wines are produced.

White Wines Versus Red Wines…

The pigmentation of the grape's skin determines the color of a wine. When white grapes are crushed, their skin, seeds, and stems are removed and the wine remains white. When red grapes (many have white insides) are crushed, their skin, seeds and stems remain with the juice. The juice then turns a variation of a "reddish" hue as the color from the grape's skins are absorbed. The grape varietal and the length of time the skins remain in contact with the grape juice assist in determining the color, flavor and tannin of the wine.

What about a Rosé?…

Making a Rosé wine is a combination of red and white wine techniques. After crushing, the winemaker leaves the skins, stems and seeds of the red grapes in contact with the juice until a desired color has been extracted. It is then processed like a white wine.

Fermentation and Beyond…

After crushing, the juice (now called must) is placed into containers for a designated period of time. Here, the yeasts mix with the natural sugar in the must. (Yeasts are tiny one-celled organisms naturally occurring on the grape skin/stem but can also be added by the winemaker.) Fermentation takes place as the yeast converts sugar into alcohol and carbon dioxide (a by-product of fermentation).

Once fermentation is complete, which usually takes anywhere from a few days to a few weeks, the wine is then commonly transferred into stainless steel tanks or oak barrels. For red wine, the juice must first be separated from the skins/seeds before it is transferred into a container. The wine then goes through a maturation phase lasting anywhere from a few weeks to several years.

Once the winemaker determines the wine is to his/her liking, it is ready for filtering and bottling. Most winemakers filter their wine, especially white wines, to remove any yeast or grape matter sediment. The wine is then bottled and sealed, usually with a cork or screw cap, and the winery's label is attached. The bottled wine is either ready to drink or is aged for a selected period of time.

This is a very basic explanation of the winemaking process, as there are numerous decisions and modifications that can be made during the production process. During a winery visit, ask the owner/winemaker for a tour and an explanation of his/her methods!

Three Major Types of Wine…

- Table wine: typically 8-15% alcohol
- Sparkling wine: typically 8-12% alcohol
- Fortified wine: typically 17-22% alcohol

Conversion Table…

1 acre = 2 to 10 tons of grapes

1 ton of grapes = 2.33 barrels

1 barrel = 25 cases

1 case = 12 bottles

1 bottle = 4-5 glasses

The Most Common Grapes and their Characteristics…

Please note: This is a brief overview, as grapes (and therefore the resultant wine) can have unique qualities all their own depending on terrior (see WINE TERMINOLOGY section) and how the wines are produced.

WHITES

Chardonnay (shar-dun-nay):

- the most common white wine and is grown worldwide
- commonly receives some "oak treatment" (via chips or barrel)
- an "unoaked" version ferments in stainless steel
- tastes from the oak: butterscotch / toasty / vanilla
- tastes from the grape: apple / pear / peach / tropical fruit

Gewürztraminer (geh-vertz-tra-mee-ner):

- can be produced from sweet to dry
- tastes: lychee fruit / overripe peach or mango / citrus
- tastes: floral, although can be quite perfumed

Muscat (moos-caht):

- possibly the oldest domesticated grape variety
- can be dry, but primarily used to make sweet dessert wine
- tastes: grapes / peach / rose petals

Pinot Gris / Pinot Grigio (pee-noh gree or pee-noh gree-jee-o):

- becoming a rival to Chardonnay as the most asked-for white wine
- usually medium bodied / crisp / produced dry
- tastes: light apple or pear / some mineral / not oaky

Riesling (reese-ling):

- often thought of as a sweet German wine (not necessarily so!)
- can be produced to be a sweet or dry wine
- often light-bodied, crisp and refreshing
- usually low to medium alcohol content
- tastes: fruity and flowery / some mineral

Sauvignon Blanc (saw-vee-nyon blonk):

- distinctive, pungent flavors and aromas
- tastes: tart apple or pear / passion fruits / citrus
- tastes: crisp and tart / grassy and herbal

Sémillon (say-mee-yohn):

- usually used to blend with another grape
- tastes: citrus / apple / pear / ripe peach

Viognier (vee-own-yay):

- a tricky grape to grow / wine should be consumed young
- medium-bodied with low acidity
- tastes: peach / apricot / mango / pineapple

REDS

Barbera (bar-bear-rah):

- low tannin, but high acidity and often blended with other grapes
- tastes when young: cherry and raspberry
- tastes when aged: a big fruit wine with plum and blackberry

Cabernet Franc (cab-er-nay frahnk):

- a genetic parent to Cabernet Sauvignon and Sauvignon Blanc
- often considered Colorado's signature grape
- used alone but primarily blended with other red grapes
- lighter in tannin than Cabernet Sauvignon
- tastes: blackcurrant and raspberry / black licorice / vegetal

Cabernet Sauvignon (cab-er-nay saw-vee-nyon):

- one of the most common red wines and grows in most climates
- higher in tannin than other reds, although blending with another red grape can reduce the tannin impact
- medium- to full-bodied and softens with aging
- tastes: blackcurrants and other dark fruits
- tastes when aged: smoke / leather / chocolate / pepper

Grenache (greh-nosh):

- primarily blended with other grapes or used in dessert wines
- a high-alcohol wine lacking tannin and color
- tastes: dark berry flavored / allspice / cinnamon

Malbec (mall-beck):

- has emerged as a major grape / wine in the southern hemisphere
- deeply colored, full-bodied with rich tannins
- tastes: plums / rich, dark red fruits / anise

Meritage (mar-it-tidge):

- not a grape, but a term indicating 2 or more grapes (out of 8 permitted) were blended using the Bordeaux style of winemaking

Merlot (mer-low):

- bottled on its own or blended with other red grapes to merge fruit flavors and/or reduce their level of tannins
- low in tannin / usually full-bodied / deep in color
- tastes: blackcurrants / plums / chocolate / earthy / spicy

Pinot Noir (pee-noh nwahr):

- can be a difficult grape to grow, harvest and produce
- low to medium tannin / medium-bodied / thin skinned
- tastes: like a blend of red fruits (cherry and raspberry) / spicy / herbal / earthy

Sangiovese (san-joe-vay-zay):

- ranges from light- to full-bodied with medium tannin
- tastes: red fruits (strawberries to tart cherry) / sometimes a nutty or smoky taste

Syrah (sih-rah):

- in Australia is spelled Shiraz (sir-rahz)
- deeply colored, full-bodied with firm tannin
- tastes: dark fruit / pepper / licorice / tar

Tempranillo (temp-rah-nee-yoh):

- not often bottled as a stand-alone grape, but used in blends
- deep color, low acidity and high in tannin
- tastes: red and dark berries / plum / herbal / earthy

Zinfandel (zin-fan-dell):

- usually produced to be consumed young
- intense fruity aromas with a "jammy" taste
- tastes: blackberry / black cherry / pepper / licorice

OTHER

Champagne:

- a sparkling wine using a variety of secondary fermentation methods to create carbonation

Dessert Wines or Port:

- a higher alcohol wine that is fortified using additional "neutral spirits" to stop the fermentation process
- very often they are quite sweet

Fruit Wines:

- a fermented alcoholic beverage using fruit instead of grapes
- usually given the name from the fruit used

Hard Cider:

- a fermented alcoholic beverage that is made from apple juice
- ranges from sweet to dry, and its appearance from cloudy to clear

Ice Wine:

- a very sweet dessert wine
- grapes are harvested frozen on the vine to allow for a higher concentration of sugar (brix)

Mead:

- an alcoholic beverage made by fermenting honey with water and yeast
- produced from sweet to dry

Sherry:

- a fortified wine made with white grapes
- two broad classes are Fino (with flor) and Oloroso (without flor)
- flor is a unique film-forming yeast

WINE AND FOOD PAIRING BASICS

We have all heard the rule "white wine with white meat and red wine with red meat." While there is a reason behind this philosophy, the most important rule is what wine YOU want to pair with what food. Wine and food pairing is an individual choice, and everyone's sense of taste is different. The five basic rules below offer you a simple guideline to follow as you begin to research your pairing preferences. You can also find extensive pairing information on the internet and through apps. So…Explore and Enjoy!

The Five Basics Rules…

Body and Balance: The key to body and balance (see WINE TERMINOLOGY) is to match lighter, mild foods with lighter wines; rich foods with rich wines; and big, flavorful foods with medium- to full-bodied wines. It is important to ensure the wine does not dominate over the food or the food overpowers the wine.

An example of a wine overpowering a food item would be pairing a Cabernet Sauvignon with a light, white fish. With this combination you would only taste the wine, as it is usually full-bodied and high in tannin. A good pairing with the fish would be a Chardonnay, Sauvignon Blanc or a dry Colorado Riesling. With these pairings, both the food and the wine would balance or complement each other, bringing out the citrus, apple, pear and/or mineral characteristics in the wine while still savoring the delicacies of the fish.

Pairing a hearty beef stew with a light-bodied, low acidity Pinot Grigio offers a prime example of a food item that is too intense for the paired wine. With this combination the meat would overpower the wine and causes the wine to feel bland or "flabby" in your mouth. A good wine to pair with a beef stew would be a Zinfandel or a Colorado Syrah. These two wines are usually medium-bodied and fruit forward, which would enhance the meat and vegetables in the stew.

Dominant Flavor: What is the main ingredient or spice in your dish? Is your dish mild, flavorful, fatty, rich, acidic? The answer to these questions will help determine what wine will pair nicely with your dish.

If you are serving chicken in a rich, cream sauce you will want to pair it with a rich wine, such as an oaked Chardonnay. If you have a red meat sauce, then a Merlot or Sangiovese could be a good choice. Here in Colorado we like to BBQ, so a hearty Cabernet Franc or Syrah from our state or a California Zinfandel pairs well. The vegetal, fruity or "jammy" flavors in the wine will help highlight the BBQ sauce. When frying or sautéing foods, such as chicken, choose a crisp, acidic wine such as a Sauvignon Blanc, Pinot Gris or dry Colorado Riesling.

Have you heard the humorous saying: "I cook with wine, and sometimes I even put it in the food?" If your recipe includes adding wine to the dish, you should use the same wine that you will be serving with the meal. And please, don't use "cooking wine" from the grocery store!

Think the Senses: The acidity and sugar in foods and the level of tannin in red wine all play a role in your pairing decisions. When I think of a high acidic food, I think of tomatoes. A high acidic food or dish needs a wine that can stand up to the sharp food flavors. Otherwise the wine will have that bland or "flabby" feeling in your mouth. Red grape varietals from Italy and Spain, as well as red blends, which are prevalent here in Colorado, can handle the job.

For sugar, the rule is: your wine should be as sweet as your dessert/food. Colorado's late-harvest or fruit wines (see GRAPE VARIETIES section) make an excellent pairing with desserts and sweet foods. What says "dessert" better than chocolate paired with a port?

Tannins are found in red wine and are useful when paired with a protein or fatty food, as it helps to cut through the fat and cleanse the palate. The most common pairing is a Cabernet Sauvignon with a steak.

Higher Alcohol and Spicy: There are two important rules to remember when dealing with spicy foods: alcohol intensifies spice and a sweeter wine cools down a spicy food. A high alcohol, full-bodied, high tannin wine actually makes spicy food seem hotter in your mouth. Therefore, a sweet or off-dry Gewürztraminer or Riesling would be a good choice to lessen the spice.

Go Native: The best example I can offer is Vinho Verde, a grape and wine from Portugal. Before traveling to Portugal I was not a fan of the country's common grape, as it was a little too sweet and effervescent for my liking. Yet while visiting, I discovered it was the perfect wine to complement the local cuisine. It was also a perfect, refreshing beverage on a hot, humid day.

Chefs use local food recipes to complement the grapes grown in a particular region, so think about the origin of your food and investigate the grapes grown in that area. A few examples would be tomatoes/pasta with Sangiovese from Italy, an apple/pork dish with Riesling from Germany and salmon with Pinot Noir from Oregon. Delicious!

WINE TERMINOLOGY

ACIDITY: A taste factor in white wines more than red. A high amount of acidity feels crisp, tart or sour, and low acidity feels soft or "flabby." Your mouth usually salivates with acidity. See Tannin.

AGING: Holding wine to potentially improve the quality; typically in an oak barrel, stainless steel tank and/or bottle. **Aging time** depends on many factors since some wines should be consumed "young" while others improve with age.

ALCOHOL CONTENT: Determined by the sugar level in the grape juice and to some extent the yeast during fermentation. See GRAPE VARIETIES section for more information.

AROMA: What your nose smells or perceives from a "young" wine and is related to the grape variety or varieties in the wine. See Bouquet.

ASTRINGENT: An astringent wine will cause the mouth to pucker, may taste bitter or harsh and is produced by the tannin in grape skins. Red wines have varying degrees of astringency.

AVA: Stands for American Viticultural Area, which is a designated geographic area given certain distinction for growing grapes. Colorado has two – Grand Valley and West Elks; the United States has over 230.

BALANCE: A combination of wine components (acidity, tannin, fruit, body and alcohol) and how well they work (or don't work) together.

BLEND: A wine made from more than one grape varietal.

BLIND TASTING: Where the taster knows nothing about the wine in the glass. **Double-Blind Tasting** – neither the taster nor the pourer know anything about the wine in the glass. Primarily used for competition.

BODY: The perceived weight, density or thickness in how the wine feels in your mouth. Wines are described as light-, medium- or full-bodied.

BOUQUET: The complex and multi-layered scents on the nose; developed from maturation and aging in the bottle. See Aroma.

BREATHING: Pouring a bottle of wine into another container to allow it to "breathe" and mix with air; **decanting**.

BRIX: (pronounced bricks) A measurement of sugar content in the grapes. On average, grapes have 0% brix in June and +20% at harvest time.

COLOR: The tint or hue a wine has; this can vary from almost clear to deep golden for whites and cherry, purple, ruby or brick for reds. See TASTING section for more information.

COMPLEXITY: The more complex a wine is the more constantly revealing of different flavors and characteristics you continue to taste.

CORKED: A term used to describe a tainted wine, which produces an off smell and/or taste; a bad bottle is said to be "corked".

CRISP: A term used to describe a sense or taste, referring to a tart, refreshing acidity in the wine.

CRUSH: A term used to describe the process of crushing grapes; usually done by a machine and not with your feet!

DEPTH: A subjective measurement of how "dimensional" a wine is on your palate. See Complexity.

DRY WINE: A wine that has little or no sugar left after fermentation. Opposite would be **Sweet Wine**.

EARTHY: Various aromas, bouquets and/or tastes that remind you of minerals, rocks, dry leaves or soil; can also include words such as musky, tobacco, leather, tar and burnt rubber.

ESTATE BOTTLED: A term indicating one company grew the grapes and made the wine.

FERMENTATION: A natural process that occurs when yeast comes in contact with the sugar in grapes or other fruit and converts it to alcohol.

FINISH: The impression a wine leaves in your mouth after you taste it. See Complexity.

FLIGHT: A sampling of several wines that can be organized by grape, region or vintage. This is what you normally experience at a Tasting Room. See Horizontal and Vertical Tasting.

FLORAL: A term given to aromas, bouquets and/or tastes in wine suggesting flowers.

FORTIFIED WINE: Wine containing 17-22% alcohol and created by adding additional neutral alcohol; examples are dessert, port or sherry.

FRUITY: The aroma, bouquet and/or taste of fruit in the wine; fruits include red, black, tropical, citrus, pome or drupe. See TASTING section.

GRASSY / HERBAL / VEGETAL: Aroma, bouquet and/or taste terms that implies a plant, herb or vegetable characteristic, such as hay, mint or green pepper.

HORIZONTAL TASTING: A sampling of similar wine varietals from the same vintage but from different wineries. See Flight and Vertical Tasting.

LEES: Sediment from yeast cells and/or grape matter that settles to the bottom of a wine vat or bottle. **Sur Lie** wines are bottled without filtering.

LEGS: A term used in tasting wine, where the wine swirled in a glass gives the image of "legs" or "tears". There is a correlation between "legs" and alcohol content, not quality.

LENGTH: How long the wine seems to remain on your palate after tasting. See Complexity.

MINERAL: A descriptive taste for wine; how a stone might taste in your mouth.

NEW WORLD WINES: Wines that come from anywhere other than Europe.

OAK BARREL: Used for storing wine as it matures and ages prior to bottling. An oak barrel can have a profound impact on the taste of the wine depending on where the oak tree originates, how the barrel is made and the number of uses.

OAKY: A term given to white wines (particularly Chardonnay) to indicate an aroma, bouquet and/or taste of oak. Many wineries use oak chips or oak barrels to create this taste in the wine. **Unoaked:** Wines that have not received any oak treatment.

OLD WORLD WINES: Wines from Europe.

OENOLOGY (ee-nol-o-gee): The science and study of wine and winemaking. An **Oenologist** is an expert in the field. See Vinification.

OXIDIZED: A term used to describe a flaw in wine that has been exposed to too much oxygen.

RESERVE WINES: A term used by New World Wines (or Old World selling to New World) to indicate something "special" about the wine; it is not a regulated term and therefore not considered particularly meaningful.

SOMMELIER (some-all-yeah): A trained and knowledgeable wine professional who has completed several courses of study.

SPICY: Tastes on your palate that remind you of various spices, such as black pepper, cinnamon or cloves.

STAINLESS STEEL TANK: Used for storing wine as it matures and ages prior to bottling; sometimes used as a temporary storage prior to aging the wine in an oak barrel (see Oak Barrel). Stainless steel tanks offer a winemaker a "neutral" container.

SULFITES: Used as a preservative in wine to maintain freshness and prevent oxidation, also occurs naturally during fermentation.

SWEETNESS: One of the four taste perceptions on the tongue besides SOUR, BITTER and SALTY.

TANNIN: A by-product of the seeds, stems and grapes used in red winemaking. Tannin can be a soft, velvety sensation to a bitter, overpowering feeling. Your mouth usually puckers from tannin. See Astringent and Acidity.

TERROIR (tare-wahr): A French term that cannot be exactly translated, but refers to the natural effects of land, soil, climate, growing season and conditions in a particular area or vineyard.

TYPICITY: How true the wine is to the "standard" taste for that particular grape variety.

UNOAKED: Wines that have not received any oak treatment.

VERTICAL TASTING: A sampling of wines (usually the same varietal) all from the same producer, but from different vintages. See Horizontal Tasting.

VINIFICATION: The production of taking grapes and making them into wine.

VINTAGE: The year on a wine bottle referencing the year the grapes were harvested.

VITICULTURE: The process of growing grapes.

VITIS VINIFERA: The primary grape species used for winemaking.

WINE AROMA WHEEL: A device which provides words to help explain smells and flavors in wine, beginning with general terms and branching out to more specific words. (See WineAromaWheel.com.)

WINE CLUB: A feature offered by wineries providing discounts and specials on their wines.

YEAST: A naturally occurring one-celled organism that is present on grape skins. See Fermentation.

YOUNG: A wine that is meant to be drunk with little aging.

YUCK: My word used to describe a wine that tastes terrible!

Grand Valley Region

Wine Fact

Cork was developed as a
bottle closure in the late
seventeenth-century.
It was only after this that bottles
were lain down for aging,
and the bottle shapes
slowly changed from
short and bulbous
to tall and slender.

http://www.beekmanwine.com/factsquotes.htm

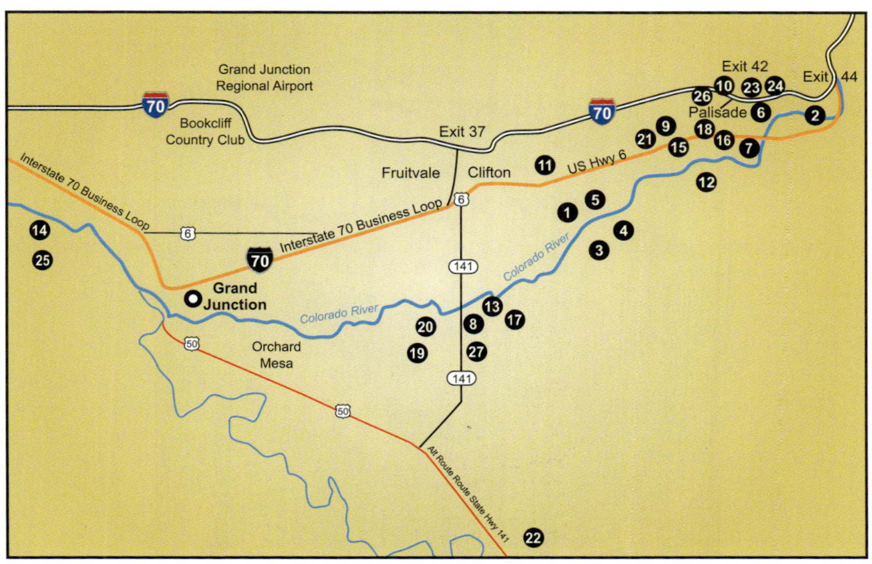

Grand Valley Region Wineries

1. Avant Vineyards
2. Canyon Wind Cellars
3. Carlson Vineyards
4. Colorado Cellars Winery
5. Colterris Wines
6. DeBeque Canyon Winery
7. Desert Moon Vineyards
8. Desert Sun Vineyards
9. Garfield Estates Vineyard & Winery
10. Grande River Vineyards
11. Graystone Winery
12. Gubbini Winery
13. Hermosa Vineyards
14. Kahil Winery
15. Maison La Belle Vie Winery
16. Meadery of the Rockies
17. Mesa Park Vineyard
18. Plum Creek Cellars
19. Ptarmigan Vineyards
20. Ram's Point Winery
21. Red Fox Cellars
22. Reeder Mesa Reds
23. St. Kathryn Cellars
24. Talon Winery
25. Two Rivers Winery
26. Varaison Vineyards & Winery
27. Whitewater Hill Vineyards

AVANT VINEYARDS

3480 E Road, Palisade, CO 81526
970-216-9908
avantvineyards.com
avantvineyards@aol.com

OWNER: Diane and Neil Guard

YEAR BEGAN OPERATION: 2008

AVERAGE CASES PRODUCED ANNUALLY: 300

WINES PRODUCED:
White: Riesling, Roussanne, Sauvignon Blanc, Viognier
Red: Cabernet Franc, Cabernet Sauvignon, Malbec, Petit Verdot, Sangiovese, Syrah, Tempranillo
Other: Sparkling-champagne

MESSAGE FROM OWNER: Award-winning, family-owned boutique winery and vineyard focusing on small batch, hand-crafted dry wines (whites, rosé, reds and sparkling) produced from our own high quality grapes. Our principal winemaking philosophy is to keep the process as basic and natural as possible, letting the character of the fruit come through. Cool night breezes sweeping off the mountains meet the hot, sunny days of this high-desert environment, helping the grapes acquire a complex concentration of aromas, colors and flavors.

Our tasting room is perfect for a relaxing picnic overlooking the Colorado River with amazing views of Mount Garfield and the Grand Mesa. We also have a Bocce court on the premises. When in season we offer delicious, estate-grown, fresh peaches.

TASTING ROOM INFORMATION: May through September, Friday from noon to 5 p.m., Saturday from 11 a.m. to 5 p.m., Sunday from noon to 4 p.m.; October through April by appointment only.

DIRECTIONS: From I-70 Westbound at Exit #44: Exit becomes Hwy 6 (G Road); turn left (south) onto 38 Road; follow main road; turn left (south) onto 36 Road; turn right (west) onto E ½ Road; turn left (south) onto 35 ½ Road; turn right (west) onto E Road, which continues as a dirt road; turn at second driveway on the right and follow signs.

From I-70 Eastbound at Exit #37: Follow I-70 Business (32 Road) south; turn left (east) onto C ½ Road; turn left (north) onto 34 ½ Road; turn right (east) onto D Road, which changes to 35 Road; turn left (west) onto E Road, which continues as a dirt road; turn at second driveway on the right and follow signs.

OTHER AMENITIES AT WINERY: Picnic area, bocce court, gorgeous views.

WINE AVAILABLE FOR PURCHASE OUTSIDE OF WINERY: No

OTHER TASTING ROOM LOCATIONS: Anita's Fruit Stand, 3819 G Road, Palisade, CO 81526.

NOTES: ______________________________

____

____

CANYON WIND CELLARS

3907 N. River Road, Palisade, CO 81526
970-464-0888
canyonwindcellars.com
info@canyonwindcellars.com

OWNER: Jay & Jennifer Christianson

YEAR BEGAN OPERATION: 1996

AVERAGE CASES PRODUCED ANNUALLY: 7,000

WINES PRODUCED:
White: Chardonnay
Red: Cabernet Franc, Cabernet Sauvignon, Malbec, Merlot, Petit Verdot
Other: 47-ten Series (White, Red, Rosé); Anemoi Wines (Apeliotes, Boreas, Lips, Notus, Zephyres); Port wine, IV

MESSAGE FROM OWNER: Planted in 1991, Canyon Wind Cellars is a family-owned, estate winery named for the mountain breezes and canyon winds that nurture the fruit on our high altitude vineyard We take pride in each and every one of our wines. Whether through focused effort, time, and hard work, or a result of years of controlled aging like our library selections, with styles from traditional and timeless to exciting and inventive—you can be sure that you will experience a wine that you won't soon forget.

TASTING ROOM INFORMATION: Daily, from 10 a.m. to 5 p.m.

DIRECTIONS: From I-70 westbound at Exit #44: Turn slightly right (southwest) onto N. River Road; winery is .5 miles ahead on left.

From I-70 eastbound at Exit #42: Turn right (south) onto Elberta Avenue (37 3/10 Road); turn left (east) onto W. 1st Street / G 4/10 Road; turn right (south) onto Main Street; turn left (east) onto E. 3rd Street, which turns into N. River Road. Winery is 1.5 miles down River Road on right.

OTHER AMENITIES AT WINERY: A boutique tasting room with gourmet foods, wine accessories, kitchen goods and home décor; outdoor picnic and wedding facilities and underground barrel cellar.

WINE AVAILABLE FOR PURCHASE OUTSIDE OF WINERY: Yes

OTHER TASTING ROOM LOCATIONS: No

NOTES: ____

____

____

____

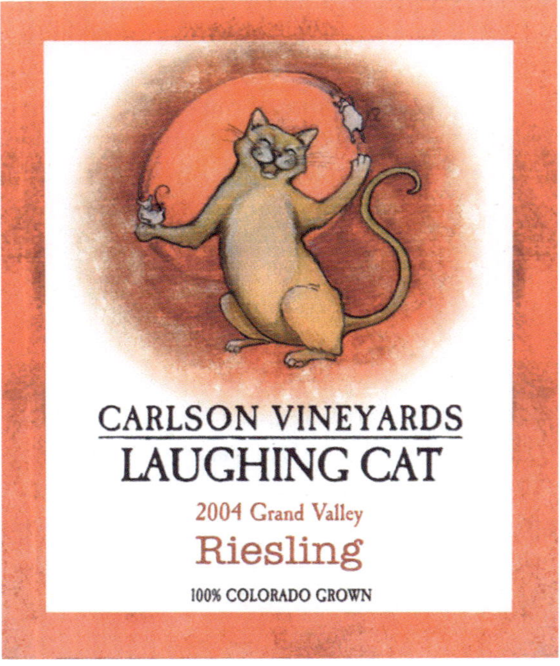

CARLSON VINEYARDS

461 35 Road, Palisade, CO 81526
970-464-5554
carlsonvineyards.com
info@carlsonvineyards.com

OWNER: Parker and Mary Carlson

YEAR BEGAN OPERATION: 1988

AVERAGE CASES PRODUCED ANNUALLY: 10,000

WINES PRODUCED:
White: Chardonnay, Gewürztraminer, Riesling
Red: Cabernet Franc, Lemberger, Merlot, Shiraz
Others: Blends called Calico, Laughing Cat Sweet Baby Red, Prairie Dog Blush and Sweet Baby White; Fruit wines; Dessert wines

MESSAGE FROM OWNER: At Carlson Vineyards, wine is not treated as the nectar of snobs! One step into the winery will show you that the Carlsons put their hearts, skill and wit into making superb wines that you will enjoy. Situated in a semi-arid landscape, this protected, high-altitude valley cut by the Colorado River produces remarkable wines. Sinfully flavorful wine grapes and fruits flourish under the care of neighboring growers. Carlson wines are known for capturing these pure, Colorado-grown fruit aromas and flavors.

In the tasting room, Parker Carlson and staff are on hand to pour samples and to chat. Notice all the medals dangling from wine bottles lining the walls. Just ask, and they will take you back into the winery to show you the winemaking process. They will also give you advice, tips and recipes on what to have with Carlson wines, and most certainly, turn you into a believer that wine is a fun adventure!

TASTING ROOM INFORMATION: Daily, from 10 a.m. to 5:45 p.m.

DIRECTIONS: From I-70 westbound at Exit #44: Exit becomes Hwy 6 (G Road); turn left (south) onto 38 Road; follow main road; turn left (south) onto 36 Road; turn right (west) onto E. 1/2 Road; turn left (south) onto 35 1/2 Road; turn right (west) onto E Road; turn left (south) onto 35 Road.

From I-70 eastbound at Exit #37: Follow I-70 Business (32 Road) south; turn left (east) onto C 1/2 Road; turn left (north) onto 34 1/2 Road; turn right (east) onto D Road, which changes to 35 Road.

OTHER AMENITIES AT WINERY: A gift shop and picnic area

WINE AVAILABLE FOR PURCHASE OUTSIDE OF WINERY: Yes

OTHER TASTING ROOM LOCATIONS: No

NOTES: ____

____

____

____

COLORADO CELLARS WINERY

3553 E Road, Palisade, CO 81526
970-464-7921 or 800-848-2812
coloradocellars.com
info@coloradocellars.com

OWNER: Richard and Padte Turley

YEAR BEGAN OPERATION: 1978

AVERAGE CASES PRODUCED ANNUALLY: 20,000 - 25,000

WINES PRODUCED:
White: Chardonnay, Gewürztraminer, Pinot Grigio, White Riesling
Red: Cabernet Sauvignon, Merlot, Syrah
Other: Blends called: Eclipse Sweet Red, Colorado Mountain Vineyards Red Table Wine, Road Kill Red; Alpenrosé; Champagne; Fruit Wines – Blackberry wine, Blueberry wine, Cherry wine, Chokecherry wine, Elderberry wine, Huckleberry wine, Peach wine, Plum wine, Pomegranate wine and Raspberry wine; Port wines and Meads

MESSAGE FROM OWNER: Colorado Cellars Winery is Colorado's oldest, largest and most award-winning winery. Founded in 1978 as Colorado Mountain Vineyards, today's brands also include Rocky Mountain Vineyards and the Orchard Mesa Wine Company. Colorado Cellars is a family-owned and operated winery, so winemaking here is truly a way of life. We grow our own grapes and fruit, keep bees for honey wine, personally make and bottle our wines and even deliver it ourselves! We are unique amongst Colorado wineries in that we are (and always have been) exclusively in the wine business. Today we continue to sell wines made under old Colorado Winery License #5, the state's oldest license still in existence!

TASTING ROOM INFORMATION: Summer, Monday through Friday from 9 a.m. to 5 p.m., Saturday and Sunday from 10 a.m. to 5 p.m. Winter, Monday through Friday from 9 a.m. to 4 p.m., Saturday from 11 a.m. to 5 p.m.

DIRECTIONS: From I-70 westbound at Exit #44: Exit becomes Hwy 6 (G Road); turn left (south) onto 38 Road; follow main road; turn left (south) onto 36 Road; turn right (west) onto E. 1/2 Road; turn left (south) onto 35 1/2 Road; turn left (east) onto E Road.

From I-70 eastbound at Exit #37: Follow I-70 Business to 32 Road; turn left (south); turn left (east) onto C 1/2 Road; turn left (north) onto 34 1/2 Road; turn right (east) onto D Road, which changes to 35 Road; turn right (east) onto E Road.

OTHER AMENITIES AT WINERY: Food, dessert and cooking products made with wine as well as facilities for meetings and weddings.

WINE AVAILABLE FOR PURCHASE OUTSIDE OF WINERY: Yes

OTHER TASTING ROOM LOCATIONS: No

NOTES: ______________________________

COLTERRIS WINES

3548 E 1/2 Road, Palisade, CO 81526
Mailing address: PO Box 1405, Palisade, CO 81526
970-464-1150
colterris.com
theresa@colterris.com

OWNER: Theresa High

YEAR BEGAN OPERATION: 2010

AVERAGE CASES PRODUCED ANNUALLY: 3,500+

WINES PRODUCED:
White: White Cabernet Sauvignon
Red: Cabernet Franc, Cabernet Sauvignon, Malbec (coming soon)
Other: None

MESSAGE FROM OWNER: Colterris Wines began operations in January 2010 and its name was derived by combining a three-letter abbreviation of Colorado "Col" with the Latin word "terris" meaning from the land. Our Cabernet Sauvignon originates primarily from grapes grown in the sun and soil of Theresa's Vineyard on East Orchard Mesa, located in Colorado's beautiful and picturesque Western Slope. Situated in the heart of the Grand Valley AVA, this unique vineyard site at 4,600' is protected by the foothills of the Grand Mesa and by close proximity to the Colorado River. This combination of high altitude sunlight and cool river nights produce a distinctively bold, red wine, rich in color, flavor and smooth tannins. I am extremely encouraged about the future potential of wines being produced here.

TASTING ROOM INFORMATION: July through September, daily, from 10 a.m. to 5 p.m. Off-season by appointment only.

DIRECTIONS: From I-70 westbound at Exit #44: Exit becomes Hwy 6 (G Road); turn left (south) onto 38 Road; follow main road; turn left (south) onto 36 Road; turn right (west) onto E 1/2 Road. We are at the junction of E 1/2 Road and 35 1/2 Road.

From I-70 eastbound at Exit #37: Follow I-70 Business (32 Road) south; turn left (east) onto C 1/2 Road; turn left (north) onto 34 1/2 Road; turn right (east) onto D Road, which changes to 35 Road; turn right (east) onto E Road; turn left (north) onto 35 1/2 Road. We are at the junction of E 1/2 Road and 35 1/2 Road.

OTHER AMENITIES AT WINERY: We provide "agritours" of the orchards, vineyards and gardens. We host weddings, feasts in the field and corporate events at our outside pavilion with 360 degree views. We have a Country Store where guests can purchase fruit, fruit products and gift items.

WINE AVAILABLE FOR PURCHASE OUTSIDE OF WINERY: Yes

OTHER TASTING ROOM LOCATIONS: No

NOTES: ____________________

____

____

____

DEBEQUE CANYON WINERY

144 Kluge Street, Bldg. 3, Palisade CO 81526
Mailing address: PO Box 1391, Palisade CO 81526
970-464-0550
debequecanyonwinery.com
debequecanyonwines@bresnan.net

OWNER: Bennett and Davelyn (Davy) Price

YEAR BEGAN OPERATION: 1997

AVERAGE CASES PRODUCED ANNUALLY: 3,500

WINES PRODUCED:
White: Chardonnay, Gewürztraminer, Riesling, Viognier
Red: Cabernet Franc, Cabernet Sauvignon, Malbec, Merlot, Syrah, Tempranillo
Other: Blend called Claret, Port wines

MESSAGE FROM OWNER: Early pioneers in the Colorado wine industry, Bennett and Davy Price designed and planted vineyards for most of the wineries in the Grand Valley. Bennett was a home-winemaker, who studied at the University of California at Davis, established friendships with a number of California winemakers and refined his winemaking style. They are best known for red wines which are full-bodied and well-aged in French oak.

Their white wines are especially noted for their fruit-forward flavors and smooth, yet slightly dry finish. As a special interest, they have crafted many Port-style wines that have won numerous awards. Recently, their daughter and grandson have joined their endeavors, making this a true, family winery.

TASTING ROOM INFORMATION: May through September, daily, from 10 a.m. to 6 p.m.; October through April, Sunday through Friday from noon to 5 p.m., Saturday from 10 a.m. to 5 p.m. Also available by appointment.

DIRECTIONS: From I-70 at Exit #42: Head south on Elberta Avenue (37 3/10 Road); turn left (east) onto 1st Street; turn right (south) onto Kluge Street; turn right (west) onto 2nd Street (just before RR tracks) to Building #3 on the right.

OTHER AMENITIES AT WINERY: Wine-related gifts. The tasting room, located inside the Winery, is available for special barrel tastings.

WINE AVAILABLE FOR PURCHASE OUTSIDE OF WINERY: Yes

OTHER TASTING ROOM LOCATIONS: No

NOTES: ____

____

____

____

DESERT MOON VINEYARDS

Palisade, CO 81526
303-990-9463
desertmoonvineyards.com
info@desertmoonvineyards.com

OWNER: Debra Ray

YEAR BEGAN OPERATION: 2005

AVERAGE CASES PRODUCED ANNUALLY: Information not Available

WINES PRODUCED:
White: Pinot Grigio, Riesling
Red: Merlot
Other: Blend called Altitude, Port wine, Shiver (an ice-style)

MESSAGE FROM OWNER: Desert Moon Vineyards began in 2002 when we purchased a 20-acre farm in Palisade. We planted our favorite grapes – Cabernet Sauvignon, Merlot and a little Syrah - and, in 2004, produced our first vintage of 50 cases.

We are excited to make wine in the highest altitude, and perhaps, most unforgiving climate in the United States. We believe the sun, soil and climate combine to produce wines of intense character.

TASTING ROOM INFORMATION: Not open to the public

DIRECTIONS: N/A

OTHER AMENITIES AT WINERY: N/A

WINE AVAILABLE FOR PURCHASE OUTSIDE OF WINERY: No

OTHER TASTING ROOM LOCATIONS: No

NOTES: ____

____

____

____

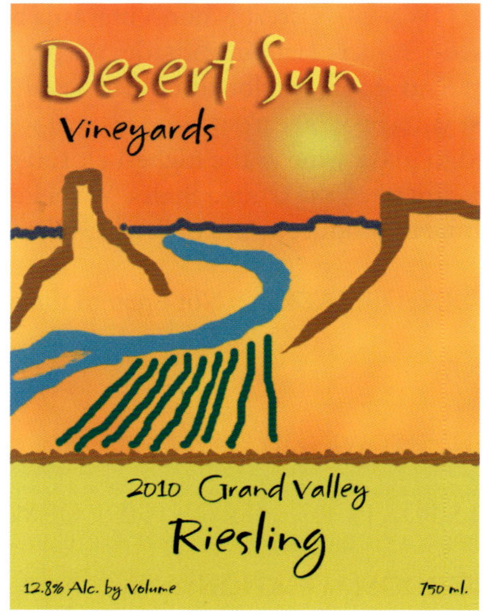

DESERT SUN VINEYARDS

3230 B 1/2 Road, Grand Junction, CO 81503
970-434-9851
desertsunvineyards.com
doug@desertsunvineyards.com

OWNER: Doug and Kathryn Hovde

YEAR BEGAN OPERATION: 2008

AVERAGE CASES PRODUCED ANNUALLY: 50

WINES PRODUCED:
White: Chardonnay, Riesling
Red: Cabernet Sauvignon, Zinfandel
Other: None

MESSAGE FROM OWNER: Desert Sun Vineyards is a small, family-owned vineyard and winery. We take advantage of the wonderful terroir that the Grand Valley has, and make high quality wines. Please come and enjoy!

TASTING ROOM INFORMATION: May through November, Friday through Sunday from 11 a.m. to 5 p.m.

DIRECTIONS: From the intersection of I-70 and Exit #37: Head south on I-70 Business (Hwy 141); turn left (south) onto 32 Road; turn left (east) onto B 1/2 Road.

OTHER AMENITIES AT WINERY: N/A

WINE AVAILABLE FOR PURCHASE OUTSIDE OF WINERY: Yes

OTHER TASTING ROOM LOCATIONS: No

NOTES: ____

____

____

____

GARFIELD ESTATES VINEYARD AND WINERY

3572 G Road, Palisade, CO 81526
970-464-0941
garfieldestates.com
info@garfieldestates.com

OWNER: Curt and Dee Barratt

YEAR BEGAN OPERATION: 2000

AVERAGE CASES PRODUCED ANNUALLY: 1,500

WINES PRODUCED:
White: Fumé Blanc, Moscato, Viognier
Red: Cabernet Franc, Syrah
Other: Red Table Blend; Vin de Glace (Ice wine); Vin au Chocolat (Port wine)

MESSAGE FROM OWNER: Our first estate vineyards were planted in early 2000 and since then, Garfield Estates Vineyard & Winery has been committed to a simple approach. Produce high quality wines using Colorado Estate grown grapes that appeal to a broad spectrum of wine lovers. This translates to growing the highest quality grapes possible using sustainable methods in the vineyard and applying passion and know how to turning those grapes into drinkable, approachable wines.

Making that possible requires successful execution in all aspects of the winemaking business. Good grapes come from the unique Colorado growing conditions or *terroir*, including close to the same degree days as Napa Valley – bright, high-altitude sunny days and cool evenings. Taking solid grapes and making delicious wine also requires a capable facility, good equipment and knowledgeable wine making. Our scale offers the opportunity to handcraft each wine to insure adherence to our philosophy of high quality, approachability and broad appeal.

We are a family owned and operated business that flows from a shared passion for the living thing that is wine. We thrive on offering to share our passion and offer hospitality to our guests and wine club members. Please be assured that you will always be at home when visiting Garfield Estates Vineyard & Winery.

TASTING ROOM INFORMATION: Daily, from 11 a.m. to 5 p.m.

DIRECTIONS: From the intersection of I-70 and Exit #42 in Palisade: Head south on Elberta Avenue (37 3/10 Road); turn right (west) onto G 4/10 Road; follow this road until it merges with 35 8/10 Road; turn left (south); at G Road turn right (west); the winery will be on your right (north side).

OTHER AMENITIES AT WINERY: Vineyard tours available upon request.

WINE AVAILABLE FOR PURCHASE OUTSIDE OF WINERY: Yes

OTHER TASTING ROOM LOCATIONS: No

NOTES: ____

____

____

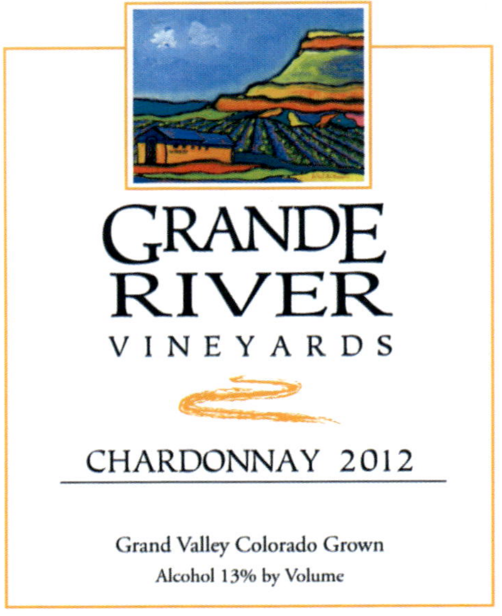

GRANDE RIVER VINEYARDS

787 N. Elberta Avenue, Palisade, CO 81526
Mailing address: PO Box 129, Palisade, CO 81526
970-464-5867
granderiverwines.com
info@granderiverwines.com

OWNER: Stephen and Naomi Smith

YEAR BEGAN OPERATION: 1990

AVERAGE CASES PRODUCED ANNUALLY: 5,000

WINES PRODUCED:
White: Chardonnay, Riesling, Sauvignon Blanc, Viognier
Red: Cabernet Franc, Cabernet Sauvignon, Malbec, Merlot, Petit Verdot, Syrah
Other: Blends called Meritage White and Meritage Red, Sweet Red, Desert Blush, Port wine and Late Harvest Viognier (dessert wine)

MESSAGE FROM OWNER: Grande River Vineyards started planting grapes in 1987, when there were only three wineries in Colorado, and produced our first vintage in 1990, becoming Colorado's fifth winery. We were Colorado's largest grape grower until selling much of our farming operation to local fruit growers in 2006.

We make wines from the classic European wine varieties in traditional styles. Our wines have won hundreds of awards in regional, national and international competitions. We consider ourselves to be the Gateway to Colorado's Wine Country, a good place to start your wine country tour! We are a Premium Winegrowing Estate as many of our wines are estate grown, produced and bottled, and all wines are made from Colorado-grown grapes. We are also Colorado's Solar Powered Winery.

Come visit our old-world-style tasting room and try some of our delicious wines, stroll through our demonstration vineyard and taste the different varieties of grapes, join us for a concert, host an event or join our wine club. You can also visit us online where you can place orders for shipment to over 20 states.

TASTING ROOM INFORMATION: Daily, from 9:00 a.m. to 5:00 p.m.

DIRECTIONS: From I-70 at Exit #42: Head south on Elberta Avenue (37 3/10 Road); turn right (west) at Grande River Drive; we are on the left under the large sign.

OTHER AMENITIES AT WINERY: We have facilities for small group meetings, catered dinners (no restaurant but two kitchens) in our cellar and an outdoor venue for concerts or weddings.

WINE AVAILABLE FOR PURCHASE OUTSIDE OF WINERY: Yes

OTHER TASTING ROOM LOCATIONS: No

NOTES: ____

____

____

____

____

GRAYSTONE WINERY

3352 F Road, Clifton, CO 81520
970-434-8610
graystonewines.com
sales@graystonewines.com

OWNER: Lynn and Vaughn Goebel

YEAR BEGAN OPERATION: 2001

AVERAGE CASES PRODUCED ANNUALLY: 1,000 - 2,000

WINES PRODUCED:
White: None
Red: None
Other: Ruby Red Port and White Port

MESSAGE FROM OWNER: A small boutique-style winery, Graystone specializes in Port, and is the only Port House in Colorado. It is named for the gray, majestic shale bluffs which surround the Grand Valley and Colorado River, and are still home to herds of wild horses. Try our quality dessert Ports, which have consistently won gold and double gold medals in both national and international wine competitions.

TASTING ROOM INFORMATION: Daily, Monday through Saturday from 10 a.m. to 5 p.m., Sunday from 11 a.m. to 5 p.m.

DIRECTIONS: From I-70 and Exit #37: Head south on Business Hwy 70; turn left (east) onto Hwy 6 (F Road); stay on Hwy 6 past 33 3/8 Road; just after 33 3/8 Road, turn right (east) onto F Road, where Hwy 6 and F Road separate.

OTHER AMENITIES AT WINERY: Gift shop; venue for small events

WINE AVAILABLE FOR PURCHASE OUTSIDE OF WINERY: Yes

OTHER TASTING ROOM LOCATIONS: No

NOTES: ______________________________

____

____

____

GUBBINI WINERY

3697 F Road, Palisade, CO 81526
970-464-5608 or 970-270-7185
Website: N/A
gubbiniwinery@aol.com

OWNER: Linda Lee Gubbini

YEAR BEGAN OPERATION: 2008

AVERAGE CASES PRODUCED ANNUALLY: Information not Available

WINES PRODUCED:
White: Chenin Blanc/Riesling, Moscato, Pinot Gris, Sauvignon Blanc
Red: Italian Reds, Malbec, Merlot, Pinot Noir, Shiraz, Tempranillo, Zinfandel
Other: Fruit wines – Apple, Blueberry, Cherry, Peach, Pomegranate and Strawberry; Dessert wines

MESSAGE FROM OWNER: It all started in 1990 with the purchase of a stone fruit orchard and homestead that was re-cultivated in 1999 into what is now Horse Mountain Vineyards. After extensive research of grape varietals, Syrah and Riesling were selected as the most compatible for the Palisade region and climate. After many seasons of learning the subtleties of grape cultivation, the yields improved and became recognized for their high quality. Presently, the grapes are being purchased and made into award-winning wines by prominent Front Range winemakers.

Being full-blooded Italian, Linda Lee Gubbini had the passion to begin producing wines under her own unique label. In 2011, Gubbini Winery opened its doors and welcomed its first guests to a home-style tasting room, which makes one feel as though they just stopped by a friend's house for a glass of wine. Gubbini Winery is able to offer a wide range of wines, and future plans include producing its own estate wines from Horse Mountain Vineyard grapes. Growing grapes and producing wine is an adventure and labor of love. Gubbini Winery welcomes all to enjoy the wine and hospitality in its tasting room in Palisade.

TASTING ROOM INFORMATION: April through October, Saturday and Sunday from 11 a.m. to 6 p.m.; November, February and March from noon to 5 p.m.; Open during the week year-round by appointment.

DIRECTIONS: From the intersection of I-70 and Exit #42 in Palisade: Head south on Elberta Avenue (37 3/10 Road); turn left (east) onto W. 8th Street/Hwy 6; turn right (south) onto 38 Road and travel 2 miles on Fruit & Wine Trail. Located on south side of F Road.

OTHER AMENITIES AT WINERY: Wine-related merchandise; vineyard tours by appointment. Bring your lunch and relax with a glass of wine in the beautiful vineyard.

WINE AVAILABLE FOR PURCHASE OUTSIDE OF WINERY: No

OTHER TASTING ROOM LOCATIONS: No

NOTES: ____

____

____

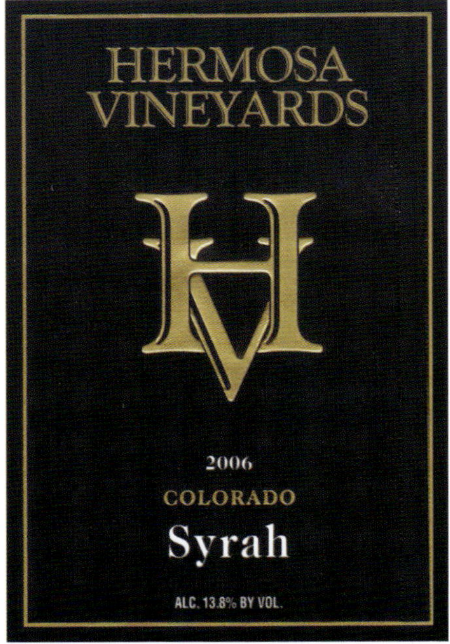

HERMOSA VINEYARDS

3269 3/4 C Road, Palisade, CO 81526
970-640-0940
hermosavineyards.com
hermosavineyards@aol.com

OWNER: Kenn Dunn

YEAR BEGAN OPERATION: 2001

AVERAGE CASES PRODUCED ANNUALLY: Information not Available

WINES PRODUCED:
White: Chardonnay, Gewürztraminer, Muscat, Riesling, Rkatsiteli, Viognier
Red: Cabernet Franc, Cabernet Sauvignon, Malbec, Merlot, Syrah
Other: Dessert wine

MESSAGE FROM OWNER: In 2001, after years of growing premium grapes for other wineries in Colorado, Kenn Dunn founded Hermosa Vineyards, LLC, a Limited Colorado Winery. Located in the Grand Valley, the winery is dedicated to handcrafting the finest wine from grapes grown in the high mountain desert of western Colorado. All of our wines are produced in very limited quantities. Our goal is not to be one of the biggest wineries, but one of the very best. With some excellent wineries located in Colorado, who are producing premium wines, we are in good company!

TASTING ROOM INFORMATION: Daily, usually from 11 a.m. to 5 p.m. or by appointment.

DIRECTIONS: From I-70 and Exit #37: Head south on I-70 Business (32 Road); turn left (east) onto C Road; at 3269 C Road, follow winery signs.

OTHER AMENITIES AT WINERY: Picnic tables

WINE AVAILABLE FOR PURCHASE OUTSIDE OF WINERY: No

OTHER TASTING ROOM LOCATIONS: No

NOTES: ____

____

____

____

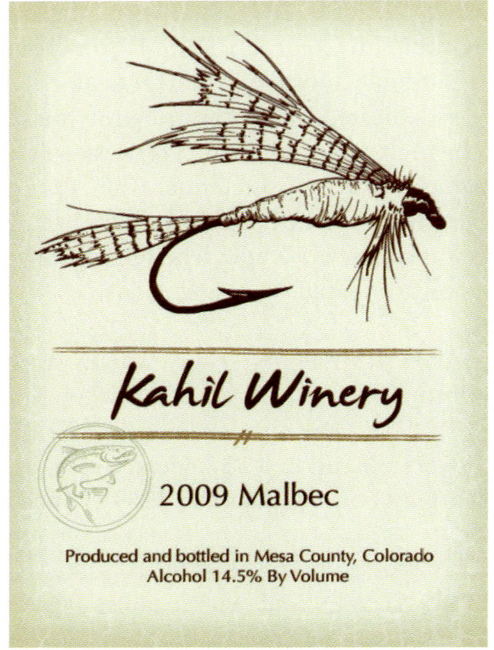

KAHIL WINERY

2087 Broadway, Grand Junction, CO 81507
970-640-3541
Website: coming soon
kahilwinery@hotmail.com

OWNER: Tyrel and Kathryn Lawson

YEAR BEGAN OPERATION: 2010

AVERAGE CASES PRODUCED ANNUALLY: 1,000

WINES PRODUCED:
(Adding other varietals over the next few years)
White: Pinot Gris
Red: Malbec
Other: None

MESSAGE FROM OWNER: Owner and winemaker, Tyrel Lawson is a Grand Valley native. Possessing a background in farming and ranching, he began working in the vineyard at Two Rivers Winery in 2004 and took over as winemaker in 2008. The initial setup of Kahil Winery began in 2009, as its first wine - a Malbec - was produced. Currently, Kahil Winery has four acres planted, which are divided between Malbec, Pinot Gris and Pinot Noir, in Eckert, Colorado. Another two acres of Malbec will be planted in 2012 in the Grand Valley.

The Malbec is a full-bodied red wine, that is fruit forward and approachable, and has the structure to pair well with food, but can be enjoyed on its own. The Pinot Gris is produced in a slightly non-traditional style, leaving a slight residual sugar and maintaining quite a bit of citrus, peach and tropical fruit on both the nose and palate. It is a great wine for everything, from the backyard summer BBQ to complementing the Thanksgiving turkey. Kahil Winery strives to produce small batch, high quality wines, that will hopefully showcase that there are good wines being produced in Colorado!

TASTING ROOM INFORMATION: By appointment only

DIRECTIONS: From the intersection of I-70 and Exit #28 (Redlands Parkway): Head south on Redlands Parkway; turn right (northwest) onto Broadway/Hwy 340. The winery is 2 miles up the road on left. (Note: GPS users should use Hwy 340 rather than Broadway.)

OTHER AMENITIES AT WINERY: N/A

WINE AVAILABLE FOR PURCHASE OUTSIDE OF WINERY: Yes

OTHER TASTING ROOM LOCATIONS: No

NOTES: ____

____

____

____

MAISON LA BELLE VIE WINERY

3575 G Road, Palisade, CO 81526
970-464-4959
maisonlabellevie.com
frenchy1972@gmail.com

OWNER: John Barbier and Garry Wright

YEAR BEGAN OPERATION: 2004

AVERAGE CASES PRODUCED ANNUALLY: 1,000

WINES PRODUCED:
White: None
Red: Cabernet Sauvignon, Merlot, Syrah
Other: Bordeaux-style reds and blends, Dessert wine, Walnut Port, Vin de Peche (Ice wine)

MESSAGE FROM OWNER: My name is John Barbier, and I am French. I have been in the food and wine industry for over 25 years. My family has been in the industry for many generations, in the Loire Valley in France.

In addition to being a winemaker, I am a chef and love to cook and show my customers that we have much to offer in Palisade, Colorado. Our wines are very authentic and we even use a recipe handed down through several generations.

We "dry farm" and do not use any chemicals in the vineyards. We are still stomping grapes with our feet and do everything by hand. We use only French oak to age our wines. Our venue is very welcoming, so please come and enjoy a unique experience at Maison la Belle Vie, which means "house of the beautiful life."

TASTING ROOM INFORMATION: Summer, daily, from 11 a.m. to 6 p.m.; Other times by appointment only.

DIRECTIONS: From the intersection of I-70 at Exit #42: Head south on Elberta Avenue (37 3/10 Road); turn right (west) onto G 4/10 Road; follow this road until it merges with 35 8/10 Road; turn left (south); at G Road turn right (west); the winery will be on your left (south side).

OTHER AMENITIES AT WINERY: Outdoor patio and dining under the willows; wine dinners, weddings and other events at Amy's Courtyard.

WINE AVAILABLE FOR PURCHASE OUTSIDE OF WINERY: Yes

OTHER TASTING ROOM LOCATIONS: No

NOTES: ______________________________

____

____

____

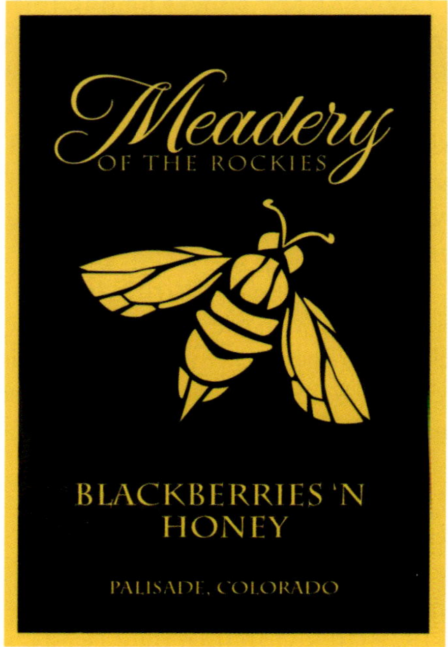

MEADERY OF THE ROCKIES

3701 G Road, Palisade, CO 81526
970-464-7899
meaderyoftherockies.com
glennf@talonwinebrands.com

OWNER: Glenn and Natalie Foster

YEAR BEGAN OPERATION: 1996

AVERAGE CASES PRODUCED ANNUALLY: 5,000

WINES PRODUCED:
White: None
Red: None
Other: Meads called King Arthur, Lancelot, Guinevere, Camelot, Apricots 'n Honey, Peaches 'n Honey, Strawberries 'n Honey, Cherrie's 'n Honey, Raspberries 'n Honey, Blackberries 'n Honey, Raspberry Chocolate Satin, Blackberry Satin, Chocolate Cherry Satin, and Honey Shere'

MESSAGE FROM OWNER: Meadery of the Rockies is owned by Glenn and Natalie Foster, who have been involved in commercial wineries in the Grand Valley since 1995. Having founded Talon Winery in 2005, the Fosters acquired Meadery of the Rockies and St. Kathryn Cellars in 2008 in order to increase their production capacity. All wines are produced at the Meadery of the Rockies.

If you can call ahead to arrange a time, tours of the winery are available, where you will learn all about their production methods. Meadery of the Rockies offers about 15 different meads, including traditionals, melomels and fortified dessert meads.

TASTING ROOM INFORMATION: Daily, from 10:00 a.m. to 5:00 p.m.

DIRECTIONS: From I-70 and Exit #42: Head south on Elberta Avenue (37 3/10 Road); turn right (west) onto G Road. The Meadery of the Rockies will be ¼ mile down on your right.

OTHER AMENITIES AT WINERY: We have a wonderful gift shop selling honey-related items and wine paraphernalia.

WINE AVAILABLE FOR PURCHASE OUTSIDE OF WINERY: Yes

OTHER TASTING ROOM LOCATIONS: Talon Winery and St. Kathryn Cellars, 785 Elberta Avenue, Palisades, CO 81526; Honeyville Tasting Room, 33633 Hwy 550, Durango, CO 81301.

NOTES: ______________________________

____

____

____

MESA PARK VINEYARDS

3321 C Road, Palisade, CO 81526
970-434-4191
mesaparkvineyards.com
pricebooker@aol.com

OWNER: Brooke and Brad Webb, Patty and Chuck Price

YEAR BEGAN OPERATION: 2009

AVERAGE CASES PRODUCED ANNUALLY: 750

WINES PRODUCED:
White: Riesling (coming soon)
Red: Cabernet Franc, Cabernet Sauvignon, Merlot
Other: Family Reserve Red; Rosé and Port wine (coming soon)

MESSAGE FROM OWNER: Our family handcrafts premium, estate-grown red wines. Visit our estate - a beautiful vineyard of the classics: Merlot, Cabernet Sauvignon and Cabernet Franc.

TASTING ROOM INFORMATION: April through November, Thursday through Monday from 11 a.m. to 5:00 p.m.; December through March by appointment only.

DIRECTIONS: From I-70 and Exit #37: Head south on Elberta Avenue (37 3/10 Road); turn left (south) onto 32 Road; turn left (east) onto C Road.

OTHER AMENITIES AT WINERY: We can accommodate small groups of up to 35 people and have ample space for picnics.

WINE AVAILABLE FOR PURCHASE OUTSIDE OF WINERY: Yes

OTHER TASTING ROOM LOCATIONS: No

NOTES: ____

____

____

____

PLUM CREEK CELLARS

3708 G Road, Palisade, CO 81526
970-464-7586
plumcreekwinery.com
plumcreekwinery@att.net

OWNER: Sue Phillips

YEAR BEGAN OPERATION: 1984

AVERAGE CASES PRODUCED ANNUALLY: Information not Available

WINES PRODUCED:
White: Chardonnay, Pinot Gris, Riesling, Sauvignon Blanc
Red: Cabernet Franc, Cabernet Sauvignon, Merlot, Sangiovese, Syrah
Other: Blends called Palisade Red, Palisade Festival, Palisade Rosé, Grand Mesa Meritage

MESSAGE FROM OWNER: Plum Creek Winery offers an authentic sense of Colorado terroir. Sourcing grapes from local vineyards has been our touchstone, since Doug and Sue Phillips founded the winery in 1984. Plum Creek has held true to this commitment of making Colorado-grown wines for more than 31 vintages, all the while maintaining a standard of excellence and consistency.

In addition to using grapes from small Western Slope growers, Plum Creek also farms more than 55 acres, planted in Colorado's high-altitude wine-growing regions centered in Palisade and Paonia. Plum Creek features a variety of wines sure to appeal to all tastes: Sauvignon Blanc, Cabernet Sauvignon, Chardonnay, Riesling, Merlot, and our premium Grand Mesa Meritage. Plum Creek is also famed for the Palisade series of wine: Festival, Palisade Rosé and Palisade Red.

We feature a knowledgeable staff in an inviting, spacious tasting room filled with fine art and antiques, along with outdoor sculpture, to enhance the wine-tasting experience.

TASTING ROOM INFORMATION: Daily, from 10 a.m. to 5 p.m.

DIRECTIONS: From the intersection of I-70 and Exit #42 in Palisade: Head south on Elberta Avenue (37 3/10 Road); turn right (west) onto G Road/Hwy 6. Look for the winery's "Chardonnay Chicken" sculpture at the entrance.

OTHER AMENITIES AT WINERY: Unique gifts, wine-related merchandise, locally-made artisanal items

WINE AVAILABLE FOR PURCHASE OUTSIDE OF WINERY: Yes

OTHER TASTING ROOM LOCATIONS: Tewksbury and Company, 1512 Larimer Sreet., Denver, CO 80202

NOTES: ____

____

____

____

PTARMIGAN VINEYARDS

221 31 3/10 Road, Grand Junction, CO 81503
Mailing address: PO Box 966, Cedaredge, CO 81413
970-434-2015
stoneymesa.com
wine@stoneymesa.com

OWNER: Neal Family

YEAR BEGAN OPERATION: 1990

AVERAGE CASES PRODUCED ANNUALLY: Information not Available

WINES PRODUCED:
White: Gewürztraminer, Pinot Gris, Riesling, Glacier
Red: Merlot, Pinot Noir
Other: Red Blend (Rojo), White Blend (Blanca), Rosé

MESSAGE FROM OWNER: Riesling is King at our modern facility, which utilizes proven Old World technology with modern equipment. We incorporate gentle fruit handling, temperature-controlled fermentation and small lot production into our wines.

Since starting in 1990, Stoney Mesa Winery has become a pioneer in the production of wine grapes and winemaking in Colorado. Our first vintage was released to the public in 1993 and, since then, we are highly regarded as one of the top white wine producers in the state. In 2000 Ptarmigan Vineyards was added to our estate.

Over the past 20 years, we have grown and expanded our facilities, production and vineyards but still focus on high quality wines at a great price.

TASTING ROOM INFORMATION: Please call for hours

DIRECTIONS: From I-70 and Exit #37: Head south on Hwy 141 (32 Road); turn right (west) onto B Road; turn right (north) onto 31 3/10 Road; the winery will be on your right.

OTHER AMENITIES AT WINERY: Patio and vineyards

WINE AVAILABLE FOR PURCHASE OUTSIDE OF WINERY: No

OTHER TASTING ROOM LOCATIONS: Stoney Mesa Winery, 16199 Happy Hollow Road, Cedaredge, CO 81413

NOTES: ____

____

____

____

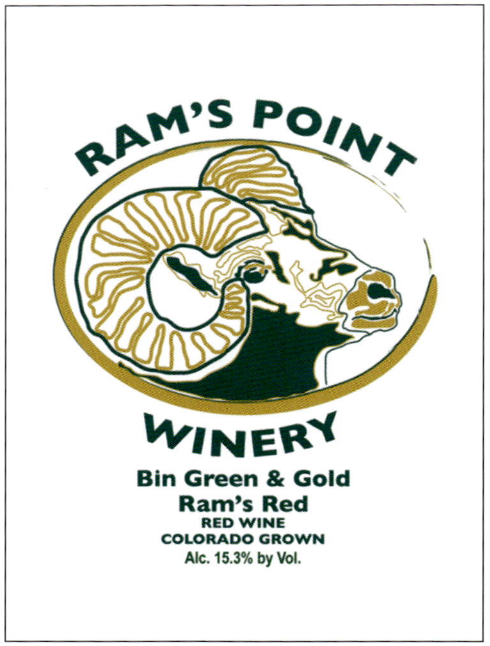

RAM'S POINT WINERY

3168 B ½ Road, Grand Junction, CO 81503
970-434-3264 Ext 201
ramspointwinery.com
info@ramspointwinery.com

OWNER: Colorado State University – Colorado Agricultural Experiment Station

YEAR BEGAN OPERATION: 2013

AVERAGE CASES PRODUCED ANNUALLY: 700

WINES PRODUCED:
White: None
Red: None
Other: Blends called: Bin Green and Gold Ram's White, Ewe Delight White, Bin Green and Gold Ram's Red, Rollicking Ram Red

MESSAGE FROM OWNER: The winery came into existence and operates as a non-profit, to further the education of Colorado State University Viticulture and Enology students. The program involves investigating the use of suitable, cold hardy varieties in blends, and performs research and outreach activities for the Colorado grape and wine industry.

The wines are blends of wines made from traditional *Vitis vinifera* culrtivars and interspecific, cold hardy cultivars. Our market demographic is primarily linked to CSU and to lovers of unique blends.

TASTING ROOM INFORMATION: None, but sales on site and through website.

DIRECTIONS: From I-70 at Exit #37: Follow Hwy 141 (32 Road) south; turn right (west) onto B ½ Road; the winery is ½ mile on B ½ Road at the Western Colorado Research Station-Orchard Mesa.

OTHER AMENITIES AT WINERY: No

WINE AVAILABLE FOR PURCHASE OUTSIDE OF WINERY: Yes

OTHER TASTING ROOM LOCATIONS: No

NOTES: ______________________________

____

____

____

RED FOX CELLARS

695 36 Road, Palisade, CO 81526
970-464-1099
redfoxcellars.com
info@redfoxcellars.com

OWNER: Sherrie and Scott Hamilton, along with our sons Chad, Kyle, Erik and daughter-in-law, Kelly

YEAR BEGAN OPERATION: 2012

AVERAGE CASES PRODUCED ANNUALLY: 800 - 1,000

WINES PRODUCED:
White: None
Red: Cabernet Franc, Cabernet Sauvignon, Merlot
Other: Red blends, Fruit wines, Hard ciders, Carbonated wine

MESSAGE FROM OWNER: Red Fox Cellars is the culmination of our family's dream to produce something with our hands. We're a family of strong opinions, but somehow we get along. There are only a handful of things we all see eye-to-eye on, and the most important one is a belief that good food and good drink can make a good day great and a bad day good. We've spent a lot of time perfecting recipes, and along with that comes a lot of experimentation. We may try and fail here and there, but we learn a lot along the way. None of us is classically trained in winemaking, and that is nothing we are ashamed of. As a matter of fact, we embrace it; it's a point of pride; it's an opportunity to be ourselves even in our wines; to take risks we see as practical that others see as crazy. There is a lot to learn from the various traditions and schools of winemaking, and we see ourselves as students of them all. We do not see our style as superior, merely enjoy our freedom to move freely between tradition and invention. We see none of the risks we take with wine as a novelty. We are out to make quality wine that is unique.

TASTING ROOM INFORMATION: Tasting Room hours vary by season; please see our website for hours.

DIRECTIONS: From I-70 at Exit #42 (Elberta Avenue): head south on Elberta Avenue; turn right (west) onto Hwy 6/G Road; turn left (southwest) onto Hwy 6/Front Road; turn right (north) onto 36 Road (over RR tracks); the winery is on your left.

OTHER AMENITIES AT WINERY: Open air tasting room with indoor and outdoor seating; picnic area; outdoor lawn games; special events throughout the year.

WINE AVAILABLE FOR PURCHASE OUTSIDE OF WINERY: Yes

OTHER TASTING ROOM LOCATIONS: No

NOTES: ____

____

____

____

REEDER MESA VINEYARDS

7799 Reeder Mesa Road, Whitewater, CO 81527
970-242-7468
reedermesawines.com
info@reedermesawines.com

OWNER: Doug and Kris Vogel

YEAR BEGAN OPERATION: 2000

AVERAGE CASES PRODUCED ANNUALLY: 1,200

WINES PRODUCED:
White: Gewürztraminer, Riesling
Red: Cabernet Franc, Cabernet Sauvignon, Petit Sirah, Petit Verdot, Syrah, Zinfandel
Other: Blends called Lands End Wild Rosé, CabSyrah, Lands End Red, Red Rocker Red; Port wine called Purple Haze.

MESSAGE FROM OWNER: Reeder Mesa Vineyards is a family-owned and operated vineyard and winery, where we strive to make your visit special. Our goal is to take the snobbery out of wine, one bottle at a time! We like to drink this stuff, not hide it away!

Savor our estate grown and bottled Riesling, as well as Cabernet Sauvignon and the very special Lands End Red. Reeder Mesa also now offers a great answer to Port, Purple Haze.

We have over 400 Wine Club members who enjoy our Quarterly Wine "Pick Up Party" featuring food, barrel tasting and local entertainment. The business is growing and the quality of our wines is improving with each vintage.

Come visit and taste our delicious, award-winning wines!

TASTING ROOM INFORMATION: Wednesday through Saturday from 10 a.m. to 6 p.m., Sunday from noon to 4 p.m. Also, by appointment.

DIRECTIONS: From the intersection of Hwy 50 and Hwy 141, south of Grand Junction: Head south on Hwy 50; turn left (east) onto Reeder Mesa Road, just past Whitewater. We are 8 miles down the road. Turn right (south) at the Winery sign and drive down the dirt road to our entry gate.

OTHER AMENITIES AT WINERY: Wine-related and other merchandise for sale.

WINE AVAILABLE FOR PURCHASE OUTSIDE OF WINERY: Yes

OTHER TASTING ROOM LOCATIONS: No

NOTES: ______________________________

____

____

____

ST. KATHRYN CELLARS

785 Elberta Avenue, Palisade, CO 81526
970-464-9288
st-kathryn-cellars.com
glennf@talonwinebrands.com

OWNER: Glenn and Natalie Foster

YEAR BEGAN OPERATION: 1999

AVERAGE CASES PRODUCED ANNUALLY: 4,700

WINES PRODUCED:
White: Pinot Grigio, Riesling
Red: None
Other: Fruit wines–Apple Blossom, Golden Pear, Cherry, Peach Passion, Concord Grape, Lavender, Strawberry Rhubarb, White Merlot, Pomegranate, Cranberry Kiss, Blueberry Bliss, Elderberry, Sweet Scarlet, and Merlot Port

MESSAGE FROM OWNER: St. Kathryn Cellars is owned and operated by Glenn and Natalie Foster, who purchased it in 2008. The Fosters have been in the wine industry since 1993, as Glenn's father founded and ran Ravenswood Winery in California for approximately 30 years.

St. Kathryn Cellars is famous for its fruit wines. Although there are a few grape wines, the most popular labels are Pomegranate, Strawberry Rhubarb, Cranberry Kiss, Blueberry Bliss, Peach Passion, and the new Lavender wine. While these wines are uncommon, they are also uncommonly delicious!

TASTING ROOM INFORMATION: Daily, from 10 a.m. to 5 p.m. During the summer, Friday and Saturday to 6 p.m.

DIRECTIONS: From I-70 at Exit #42: Head south on Elberta Avenue (37 3/10 Road). We are on the right.

OTHER AMENITIES AT WINERY: The Colorado Fudge Factory, where we offer hundreds of flavors and free tastes! A large gift shop stocked with wine paraphernalia and beautiful home décor items.

WINE AVAILABLE FOR PURCHASE OUTSIDE OF WINERY: Yes

OTHER TASTING ROOM LOCATIONS: Talon Winery, 785 Elberta Avenue, Palisade, CO 81526; Meadery of the Rockies, 3701 G Road, Palisades, CO 81526; Honeyville Tasting Room, 33633 Hwy 550, Durango, CO 81301

NOTES: ____

____

____

____

TALON WINERY

785 Elberta Avenue, Palisade, CO 81526
970-464-9288
talonwineryco.com
glennf@talonwinebrands.com

OWNER: Glenn and Natalie Foster

YEAR BEGAN OPERATION: 2005

AVERAGE CASES PRODUCED ANNUALLY: 2,000

WINES PRODUCED:
White: Chardonnay, Riesling, Viognier
Red: Cabernet Sauvignon, Merlot
Other: Blends called Wingspan White and Wingspan Red; Rosato (Rosé); Aquila, a dessert port

MESSAGE FROM OWNER: Talon Winery was founded by Glenn and Natalie Foster in 2005 when they opened a small, retail wine shop and produced a limited amount of wine in the back room. After three years, they needed to expand capacity, so they moved their operations to Palisade and acquired two other brands.

Talon Winery is dedicated to making top quality, traditional grape wines. We currently offer 10 varieties that regularly win awards for quality at national and international competitions. We hope you get a chance to stop by and enjoy free samples of our wines, homemade fudge as well as a wide variety of wine-related gifts and décor!

TASTING ROOM INFORMATION: Daily, from 10 a.m. to 5 p.m. During the summer, Friday and Saturday to 6 p.m.

DIRECTIONS: From I-70 at Exit #42: Head south on Elberta Avenue (37 3/10 Road). We are on the right.

OTHER AMENITIES AT WINERY: The Colorado Fudge Factory, where we offer hundreds of flavors and free tastes! A large gift shop stocked with wine paraphernalia and beautiful home décor items.

WINE AVAILABLE FOR PURCHASE OUTSIDE OF WINERY: Yes

OTHER TASTING ROOM LOCATIONS: St. Kathryn Cellars, 785 Elberta Avenue, Palisade, CO 81526; Meadery of the Rockies, 3701 G Road, Palisades, CO 81526; Honeyville Tasting Room, 33633 Hwy 550, Durango, CO 81301.

NOTES: ____

____

____

____

TWO RIVERS WINERY

2087 Broadway Road, Grand Junction, CO 81507
970-255-1471 or 866-312-9463
tworiverswinery.com
info@tworiverswinery.com

OWNER: Robert "Bob" and Billie Witham

YEAR BEGAN OPERATION: 1999

AVERAGE CASES PRODUCED ANNUALLY: 14,000-16,000

WINES PRODUCED:
White: Chardonnay, Riesling
Red: Cabernet Sauvignon, Merlot, Syrah
Other: Vintner's Blend, Ruby Port, Tulip (Rosé)

MESSAGE FROM OWNER: This family-operated boutique winery, offers wines from the noble varieties. Chateau deux Fleuves Vineyards (translated House on Two Rivers), encompasses 11 acres of estate-grown Chardonnay, Cabernet Sauvignon and Merlot grapes. In addition to estate-grown grapes, local grapes are purchased through contracts with other Colorado growers. The state-of-the-art winery is positioned in the center of the vineyard.

Great care and thought has been given to equip the crush area, fermentation room and cellar so that a high level of quality is maintained when taking the grapes from harvest, through fermentation, aging and bottling. While these meticulous practices have been implemented to enhance the complexity of the wine, there remains openness to innovation, which enables the winery to be responsive to its customers. This process is essential in achieving our three goals: Premium Wines, Consistency and Predictability and Customer Participation.

TASTING ROOM INFORMATION: Monday through Saturday from 10:30 a.m. to 6 p.m., Sunday from noon to 5 p.m.

DIRECTIONS: From the intersection of I-70 and Exit #28 (Redlands Parkway): Head south on Redlands Parkway; turn right (northwest) onto Broadway/Hwy 340. The winery is 2 miles up the road on left. (Note: GPS users should use Hwy 340 rather than Broadway.)

OTHER AMENITIES AT WINERY: Event Center, which can host a variety of functions and contains a fully-equipped catering kitchen. Ten upscale guest rooms are available at our Wine Country Inn featuring unique French Country décor, expanded buffet style breakfast and outstanding hospitality.

WINE AVAILABLE FOR PURCHASE OUTSIDE OF WINERY: Yes

OTHER TASTING ROOM LOCATIONS: No

NOTES: ______________________________

____

____

VARAISON VINEYARDS AND WINERY

405 W. 1st Street, Palisade, CO 81526
970-464-4928
varaisonvineyards.com
info@varaisonvineyards.com

OWNER: Ron and Kristin West

YEAR BEGAN OPERATION: 2001

AVERAGE CASES PRODUCED ANNUALLY: 12,000

WINES PRODUCED:
White: Black Moscato, Créme Brûlée Chardonnay, Montagne Doux Viognier
Red: Barbera, Bin 3115 Merlot Estate Reserve, Nebiolo Reserva, Priitivo
Other: Forbidden Fruit Hard Apple Cider, Forbidden Fruit Black Moscatorita Wine cooler

MESSAGE FROM OWNER: Varaison Vineyards and Winery is a family-owned boutique winery specializing in the production of premium quality estate wines. Located in Palisade, our state-of-the-art facility produces predominantly Old World style Burgundy, Bordeaux and Italian varietals as well as sparkling wines that are produced both method Charmat and Methode Champenoise. Varaison strives to allow the expression of the terroir unique to the Grand Valley AVA, by growing grapes that are herbicide- and pesticide-free, in support of sustainable agricultural practices.

Our company and staff are dedicated to enhancing the wine tasting experience by providing personalized education and knowledge to each valued guest. Varaison provides a distinctive venue, experience and opportunity to explore Colorado wines.

A 100-year-old Victorian tasting room and formal English rose garden offer a unique atmosphere for a relaxing and informative visit.

TASTING ROOM INFORMATION: Daily, from 10 a.m. to 5 p.m.

DIRECTIONS: From I-70 at Exit #42: Head south on Elberta Avenue (37 3/10 Road); turn left (east) onto 1st Avenue.

OTHER AMENITIES AT WINERY: The Palisade Pavilion accommodates up to 250 people for any event need and includes a catering kitchen. The Walking Gardens features over 1,600 David Austin Old English Roses. “Fire Pit Fridays” wine and food celebration every Friday at 6 p.m.

WINE AVAILABLE FOR PURCHASE OUTSIDE OF WINERY: No

OTHER TASTING ROOM LOCATIONS: No

NOTES: ______________________________

____

____

____

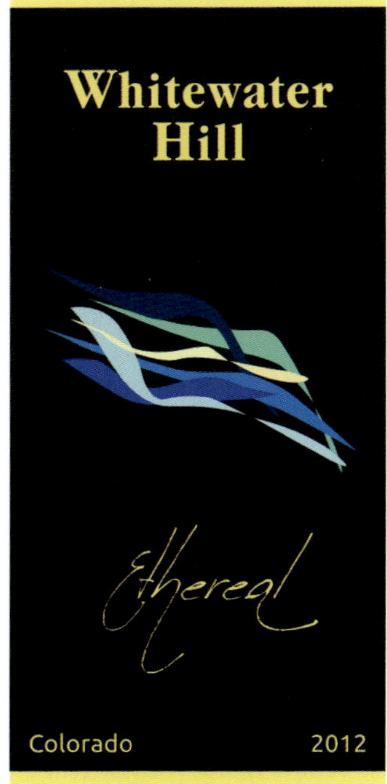

WHITEWATER HILL VINEYARDS

220 32 Road, Grand Junction, CO 81503
Mailing address: 130 31 Road, Grand Junction, CO 81503
970-434-6868
whitewaterhill.com
info@whitewaterhill.com

OWNER: Nancy Janes and John Behrs

YEAR BEGAN OPERATION: 2004

AVERAGE CASES PRODUCED ANNUALLY: 2,000

WINES PRODUCED:
White: 'Barrel Select' Chardonnay, 'No Oak' Chardonnay, Riesling
Red: Cabernet Franc, Cabernet Sauvignon, Merlot, Shiraz
Other: Blends called Ethereal and Sweetheart Red; Mélange Rosé; Ruby Classico Port-style; Riesling Icewine

MESSAGE FROM OWNER: Whitewater Hill Vineyards is a family-owned and operated vineyard and winery, located in Grand Junction, Colorado. The husband and wife team of John Behrs and Nancy Janes left the high tech industry in Boulder in 1998 to grow grapes in the Grand Valley. John concentrates on the grape growing in the summer, and helps winemaker Nancy in the cellar during the winter.

They produce ten different wine grape varieties on 24 acres in the Grand Valley, growing both for other wineries and for their own small lot production. They also make 16 different award-winning wines with Colorado grown grapes. Their wines range in style from full-bodied, dry wines, to elegant and fruity semi-sweet and dessert wines... "handgrown, handpicked, handcrafted."

TASTING ROOM INFORMATION: Summer, Monday through Friday from noon to 6 p.m., Saturday and Sunday from 10 a.m. to 6 p.m.; Winter, Friday through Sunday from noon to 6 p.m., often all week per phone message.

DIRECTIONS: From the intersection of I-70 and Exit #37 in Grand Junction: Head south on I-70 Business; turn left (south) onto Hwy 141 (32 Road). The winery is 4 miles on 32 Road.

OTHER AMENITIES AT WINERY: Wine-related merchandise

WINE AVAILABLE FOR PURCHASE OUTSIDE OF WINERY: Yes

OTHER TASTING ROOM LOCATIONS: No

NOTES: ______________________________

____

____

____

GRAND VALLEY REGION

What Else To See & Do

Allen Unique Autos Showroom & Gallery **allenuniqueautos.com**
"Beep, Beep"...take a look at this private automobile collection selected by Tammy Allen.

Bananas Fun Park **bananasfunpark.com**
Let your kids (or your inner child) go wild and unwind through mini golf, bumper boats, an inflatable play land, batting cages, go karts and laser tag.

Colorado National Monument **nps.gov/colm**
Can a rock really balance? View breathtaking scenery and captivating landscapes of towering cliffs, deep canyons, balancing rocks and giant monoliths on the 23-mile Rim Rock Drive. Find sightseeing, hiking, biking, and ranger-led programs at the Monument.

Farmers Market **townofpalisade.org & downtowngj.org**
From mid-June through mid-September, these weekly events offer much more than just produce. Visit these websites for more information.

Grand Mesa **see the Internet for various websites**
Ever been on the world's largest flat-top mountain? Grand Mesa offers a variety of outdoor activities ranging from sightseeing, hiking, biking and fishing during the summer and fall. In the winter, activities include crosscountry skiing, snowshoeing and snowmobiling. Powderhorn Mountain Resort offers downhill skiing and summer activities (www.powderhorn.com).

John Connell Math and Science Center **mathandsciencecenter.org**
Take a break from exploring wine to explore the world of science and math. This center is filled with interactive displays and exhibits for kids of all ages to explore science and math: to touch, turn, look, listen, feel, pull, adjust, try out, and question.

Museum of Western Colorado **museumofwesternco.com**

Become a paleontologist for the day at the Museum of Western Colorado and discover what this area was like years ago. There are three major museum facilities: Museum of the West, Dinosaur Journey Museum and Cross Orchards Historic Site.

- **Museum of the West** takes you back to western Colorado a thousand years ago, and includes Native American pottery, treasures from a Spanish merchant ship and a re-creation of a pioneer town.
- **Dinosaur Journey Museum** provides visitors the opportunity to examine dinosaur fossils, see a working paleontology lab and experience a simulated earthquake. Dinosaur Digs offers halfday to 5-day paleontology expeditions where you can explore for fossils at a dinosaur quarry.
- **Cross Orchards Historic Site** transports you to the early 1900s in the Grand Valley. Your experience will be enhanced by the costumed interpreters.

Outdoor Activities **trails.com**

Hike to the top of the Book Cliff Mountain's highest peak, Mt. Garfield, and be rewarded with spectacular views. Like anywhere in Colorado, the Grand Valley region offers numerous hiking and biking trails. And don't Forget, you can always bike to the wineries! Grand Junction, Fruita and Palisade all offer city parks, swimming pools and skateparks, which can be found on each city's website.

SunCrest Orchard Alpacas **suncrestorchardalpacas.net**

Need a sweater anyone? At this unique farm find out how alpaca fur is changed into fiber and manufactured into yarn.

Western Colorado Center for the Arts **gjartcenter.org**

Enjoy the arts? The Western Colorado Center for the Arts provides exhibits, displays and educational programs to promote the enjoyment and understanding of the arts.

For further information, please visit these websites:

fruitachamber.org **gjchamber.org**
visitgrandjunction.com **palisadecoc.com**

NOTES:

West Elks Region

Wine Fact

In ancient Babylon, the bride's father would supply his son-in-law with all the mead (fermented honey beverage) he could drink for a month after the wedding. Because their calendar was lunar or moon-based, this period of free mead was called the "honey month"; what we now call the "honeymoon."

http://www.weddingnight.com/advice/history-of-honeymoons.html

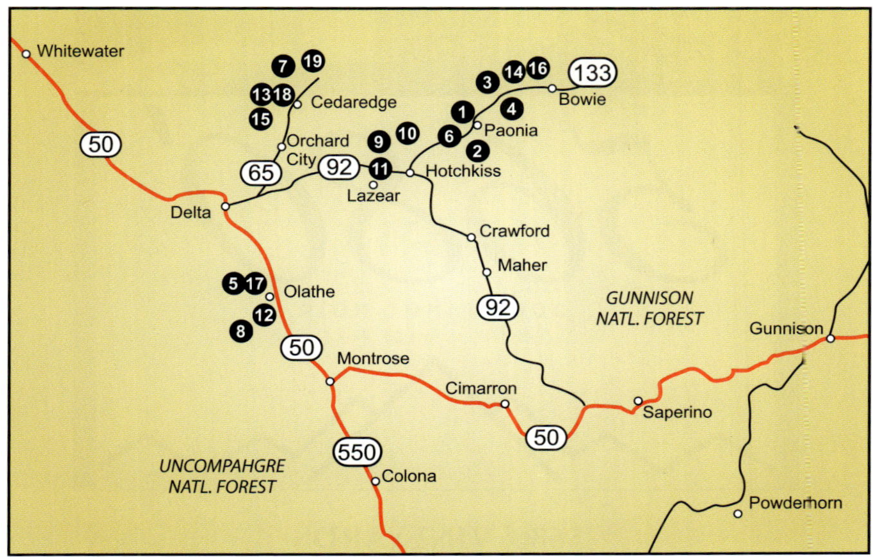

West Elks Region Wineries

1. 5680' Vineyards
2. Alfred Eames Cellars
3. Azura Cellars and Gallery
4. Black Bridge Winery
5. Cottonwood Cellars
6. Delicious Orchards
7. Edge of Cedars Farm & Winery
8. Garrett Estate Vineyards
9. Jack Rabbit Hill
10. Leroux Creek Vineyards
11. Mesa Winds Winery
12. Mountain View Winery
13. Snow Capped Cider
14. Stone Cottage Cellars
15. Stoney Mesa Winery
16. Terror Creek Winery
17. The Olathe Winery
18. Williams Cellars
19. Woody Creek Cellars

5680' VINEYARDS

14652 Peony Lane, Paonia, CO 81428
970-527-6476
website: N/A
robkimball7@hotmail.com

OWNER: Rob Kimball

YEAR BEGAN OPERATION: 2005

AVERAGE CASES PRODUCED ANNUALLY: 250-350

WINES PRODUCED:
White: Chardonnay
Red: Pinot Noir, Syrah
Other: Red blend; Dessert wine

MESSAGE FROM OWNER: Crisp mountain air, clear intense sunlight and pure water of the Colorado high country combine to provide our grapes with one of the most unique growing conditions in the world. Our vineyard sits at 5,680 feet, within the West Elks AVA, the highest recognized wine-growing elevation in the United States.

TASTING ROOM INFORMATION: By appointment only

DIRECTIONS: From the intersection of Hwy 133 and Hwy 187: Head south on Hwy 187 (Grand Avenue) through downtown Paonia; turn right (southwest) onto First Street (changes name to County Road J.75 Drive); turn right (northwest) onto Peony Lane.

OTHER AMENITIES AT WINERY: N/A

WINE AVAILABLE FOR PURCHASE OUTSIDE OF WINERY: Yes

OTHER TASTING ROOM LOCATIONS: No

NOTES: ____

____

____

____

ALFRED EAMES CELLARS

11931 4050 Road, Paonia, CO 81428
970-527-3269
alfredeamescellars.com
eames@paonia.com

OWNER: Alfred Eames

YEAR BEGAN OPERATION: 1998

AVERAGE CASES PRODUCED ANNUALLY: 1,500

WINES PRODUCED:
White: Pinot Gris
Red: Pinot Noir, Syrah, Tempranillo
Other: Red blends called Collage and Sangre del Sol

MESSAGE FROM OWNER: My Estate bottled wine is Pinot Noir. My other wines are made from grapes grown on nearby Colorado vineyards, including the blends of Cabernet Franc, Cabernet Sauvignon, Carmine, Merlot, Syrah and Tempranillo.

TASTING ROOM INFORMATION: By appointment only

DIRECTIONS: From Hwy 133 near Paonia at the Stop and Save Gas Station on Hwy 133: Turn east onto Samuel Wade Road (changes to 3rd Street); turn right (south) onto Onarga Avenue (changes to Lamborn Mesa Road); keep straight onto 4100 Road; turn right (west) onto Stewart Mesa Road; keep straight onto 4050 Road.
(map available on website)

OTHER AMENITIES AT WINERY: N/A

WINE AVAILABLE FOR PURCHASE OUTSIDE OF WINERY: Yes

OTHER TASTING ROOM LOCATIONS: Delicious Orchards, 39126 Hwy 133, Hotchkiss, CO 81419

NOTES: ____

____

____

____

AZURA CELLARS AND GALLERY

16764 Farmers Mine Road, Paonia, CO 81428
970-390-4251
azuracellars.com
azurapaonia@aol.com

OWNER: Ty and Helen Gillespie

YEAR BEGAN OPERATION: 2007

AVERAGE CASES PRODUCED ANNUALLY: 175

WINES PRODUCED:
White: Pinot Gris, Riesling
Red: Merlot, Syrah
Other: None

MESSAGE FROM OWNER: Helen and Ty Gillespie are artists and sailors. Having completed an around-the-world cruise, they have settled down to produce world class art and boutique wines at the winery in Paonia. The stunning views and extraordinary architecture of the winery combine with boutique wines and exceptional art to make a visit to Azura Cellars an unforgettable experience!

TASTING ROOM INFORMATION: Memorial Day through the end of October, daily, from 11 a.m. to 6 p.m.

DIRECTIONS: From the intersection of Hwy 133 and Hwy 187 near Paonia: Head northeast on Hwy 133; turn left (north) onto Farmers Mine Road. The winery is about 1 mile from the Hwy 133 turnoff.

OTHER AMENITIES AT WINERY: Art Gallery and a wedding venue

WINE AVAILABLE FOR PURCHASE OUTSIDE OF WINERY: No

OTHER TASTING ROOM LOCATIONS: No

NOTES: ____

____

____

____

BLACK BRIDGE WINERY

15836 Black Bridge Road, Paonia, CO 81428
970-527-6838
blackbridgewinery.com
leeb@orchardvalleyfarms.com

OWNER: Lee and Kathy Bradley

YEAR BEGAN OPERATION: 2004

AVERAGE CASES PRODUCED ANNUALLY: 1,200

WINES PRODUCED:
White: Chardonnay, Riesling
Red: Merlot, Pinot Noir
Other: Blends called Breaker Row Red, Farmers Ditch Red

MESSAGE FROM OWNER: Western Colorado's terrain and weather have produced an ideal grape–growing region for more than a century. Nationally, Colorado is considered one of the finest emerging wine areas. Here in the West Elks, Orchard Valley Farms has been supplying some of Delta County's finest wineries with grapes since 1997.

In 2005 we introduced the premier vintage of our own wines. Named for the nearby historic bridge, Black Bridge Winery produces a limited number of wines each year. Our offerings include classic reds and red blends of Pinot Noir, Merlot, Syrah and Cabernet Sauvignon, and whites of Chardonnay and Riesling. Some are big, some are fruity, and all are delicious. Our Colorado wines are made in limited quantities, so stop by to sample and purchase in our tasting room, or shop year 'round online.

TASTING ROOM INFORMATION: Memorial Weekend through Halloween, daily from 10 a.m. to 6 p.m.

DIRECTIONS: From the intersection of Hwy 133 and Hwy 187 near Paonia: Head north on Hwy 133; turn right (east) onto Black Bridge Road, which is approximately 1 mile north of Paonia.

OTHER AMENITIES AT WINERY: An outside venue, which can accommodate up to 50 people

WINE AVAILABLE FOR PURCHASE OUTSIDE OF WINERY: Yes

OTHER TASTING ROOM LOCATIONS: No

NOTES: ____

____

____

____

COTTONWOOD CELLARS

5482 Hwy 348, Olathe, CO 81425
Mailing address: PO Box 940, Olathe, CO 81425
970-323-6224
cottonwoodcellars.com
cowinelady@cs.com

OWNER: Keith and Diana Read

YEAR BEGAN OPERATION: 1994

AVERAGE CASES PRODUCED ANNUALLY: 3,500

WINES PRODUCED:
(Note: Not all wines are produced annually)
White: Chardonnay, White Pinot Noir
Red: Cabernet Franc, Cabernet Sauvignon, Reserve Cabernet Sauvignon, Lemberger, Merlot, Reserve Merlot, Pinot Noir, Syrah
Other: Blend called Classic Blend

MESSAGE FROM OWNER: Owner's Keith and Diana Read retired from the Tech industry in California and started the Cottonwood Cellars winery in 1994. Keith apprenticed to a chemist in winemaking, as well as developing an extensive library on Enology and Viticulture. They planted 22.5 acres in seven varieties from 1995 to 2000 at 5,400' altitude, from which they produce approximately 3,500 cases per year. The red wines and Chardonnay (Sur Lees) are aged in a combination of new and neutral oak barrels from nine months to two years. The wines have superior quality, being well-balanced and varietal correct.

We were excited to have our 2009 Reserve Cabernet Sauvignon receive a Gold Medal at the San Francisco International Wine Competition.

TASTING ROOM INFORMATION: Memorial Day weekend through October, Wednesday through Saturday from 11 a.m. to 5:30 p.m.; April through Memorial Day and November through December, Friday and Saturday from 11 a.m. to 5 p.m. Closed January through March, except by appointment only.

DIRECTIONS: From the intersection of Hwy 50 and Hwy 348 in Olathe: Head west on Hwy 348. Winery is 3.4 miles on the right side.

OTHER AMENITIES AT WINERY: Event facilities in tasting room and barrel room (75 people), front lawn (125 sit down) or 300 people for weddings, receptions, reunions. We also sell gift items.

WINE AVAILABLE FOR PURCHASE OUTSIDE OF WINERY: Yes

OTHER TASTING ROOM LOCATIONS: Alpine Floral, 1414 Hawk Pkwy, Montrose, CO 81401 and The Designer's Vault, 214 8th Street #17, Glenwood Springs, CO 81601

NOTES: ____

____

____

____

DELICIOUS ORCHARDS
Home of Big B's Juices and Cider

39126 Hwy 133, Hotchkiss, CO 81419
Mailing address: PO Box 2012, Hotchkiss, CO 81419
970-527-1110
bigbs.com
info@bigbs.com

OWNER: Jeff and Tracey Schwartz and Seth Schwartz

YEAR BEGAN OPERATION: 2009

AVERAGE CASES PRODUCED ANNUALLY: Information not Available

WINES PRODUCED:
White: None
Red: None
Other: Ciders called: Cherry Daze, Harvest Apple, Lazy Daze Lemonade and Orchard Original; Seasonal Ciders called: Harvest Apple Spice and Pear Hill; Premium Series Ciders called: Bourbon Barrel-Aged Pommeau, Chester Hoppearcot, Grizzly Brand, One Night Fruit Stand, Pear Supply and Sommerset

MESSAGE FROM OWNER: We produce a traditional, still farmhouse-style dry cider, made with 100% organic cider apples. It is handcrafted and all naturally fermented in small batches. A bouquet of apple blossom mingles with the subtle sweetness of apple and floral flavors. Our cider is an excellent match on a hot summer night….Ah, who are we kidding? It tastes great and we drink it all the time!

Delicious Orchards, the home of Big B's Juices and Cider, has a beautiful farm store with great local organic products, a café serving delicious food made from local ingredients and a campground nestled in the orchard. Additionally, guests can come by and hand pick organic cherries, pears, peaches and apples. Delicious Orchards is proud to support local, sustainable agricultural and land stewardship.

TASTING ROOM INFORMATION: May through November, daily from 8 a.m. to 6 p.m.

DIRECTIONS: Located on Hwy 133 one mile west of Paonia

OTHER AMENITIES AT WINERY: A café featuring local products, an organic farm stand, camping, special events and U-Pick.

WINE AVAILABLE FOR PURCHASE OUTSIDE OF WINERY: Yes

OTHER TASTING ROOM LOCATIONS: No

NOTES: ____

____

____

____

2014

LANDOT NOIR

vin rouge

Edge of Cedars Farm & Winery

COLORADO

12.5% ALC./VOL. 750 ml

EDGE OF CEDARS FARM & WINERY

250 SW 7th Street, Cedaredge, CO 81413
Mailing address: PO Box 224, Cedaredge, CO 81413
970-623-9189
edgeofcedarsfarm.com
edgeofcedarsfarm@gmail.com

OWNER: Larry Naslund

YEAR BEGAN OPERATION: 2014

AVERAGE CASES PRODUCED ANNUALLY: 100

WINES PRODUCED:
White: Chardonnay, Gewürztraminer, Vidal Blanc
Red: Cynthiana, Landot Noir, Sweet Concord
Other: None

MESSAGE FROM OWNER: Owner and chief winemaker, Larry Naslund, has been making home-style wines since the 1970s until getting serious about five years ago. Because of its small size, just over one acre, an eco-tour is available and allows visitors a quick inside look at a working farm featuring not just the vineyard but lavender, coneflower, elderberry, calendula (marigold), walnut and other growing species, which are for sale as well.

The featured wine here at the foot of the Grand Mesa is Landot Noir, a French/American cultivar developed in France by old Pierre Landot and brought to the Americas in the 1950s. The berries are deep purple throughout, uniquely flavored and make a deep red, fruity, well-balanced wine that is unforgettable in its characteristics.

Vidal Blanc, another French/American varietal, Norton Cynthiana (deep red, purely American, if not indigenous) and a rare, sweet Concord wine rounds out the unique possibilities here at Edge of Cedars Farm & Winery.

TASTING ROOM INFORMATION: By appointment only

DIRECTIONS: From Hwy 65 (Grand Mesa Drive) in downtown Cedaredge: Turn left (west) onto W. Main Street; turn left (south) onto SW 7th Street.

OTHER AMENITIES AT WINERY: Lambert cherries, walnuts, elderberries, lavender and coneflower for sale.

WINE AVAILABLE FOR PURCHASE OUTSIDE OF WINERY: NO

OTHER TASTING ROOM LOCATIONS: NO

NOTES: ____

____

____

____

GARRETT ESTATE CELLARS

53582 Falcon Road, Olathe, CO 81425
Mailing address: 53716 Falcon Road, Olathe, CO 81425
970-901-5919
garrettestatecellars.com
mitch@garrettestatecellars.com

OWNER: Dave and Pam Garrett

YEAR BEGAN OPERATION: 2003

AVERAGE CASES PRODUCED ANNUALLY: 4,200

WINES PRODUCED:
White: Chardonnay, Gewürztraminer, Pinot Gris, Rielsing, Viognier
Red: Cabernet Franc, Merlot, Pinot Noir, Syrah
Other: Pheasant Run Red blend; Rosé

MESSAGE FROM OWNER: Our winery is a family-run operation, started by our parents in 2003, with our first vintage being introduced in 2008. We currently grow on 35 acres and are expanding to include an additional 20 acres. Our wines are traditional and of French styling. We are working to produce exceptional, inspiring, quality Colorado wines through excellence, integrity, simplicity and cooperation.

TASTING ROOM INFORMATION: Currently we do not have a tasting room; tours by appointment only.

DIRECTIONS: N/A

OTHER AMENITIES AT WINERY: N/A

WINE AVAILABLE FOR PURCHASE OUTSIDE OF WINERY: Yes

OTHER TASTING ROOM LOCATIONS: Delicious Orchards, 39126 Hwy 133, Hotchkiss, CO 81419 and Vines Wine Bar, 19501 E. Main Street, Parker, CO 80138

NOTES: ____

____

____

____

Jack Rabbit Hill™

M&N 2009

55% Pinot Noir/45% Meunier
Grown on Jack Rabbit Hill
13.8% alc by vol
Certified Biodynamic®
Colorado

JACK RABBIT HILL

26567 North Road, Hotchkiss, CO 81419
Mailing address: PO Box 2004, Hotchkiss, CO 81419
970-361-4249
jackrabbithill.com
lance@jackrabbithill.com

OWNER: Anna and Lance Hanson

YEAR BEGAN OPERATION: 2001

AVERAGE CASES PRODUCED ANNUALLY: 1,500

WINES PRODUCED:
White: Estate Chardonnay, Riesling
Red: Pinot Noir
Other: None

MESSAGE FROM OWNER: Jack Rabbit Hill is a diversified farm. This unique property includes 22 acres of vineyards, a 12-acre hopyard, an estate winery and the Peak Spirits distillery. The property is certified organic and biodynamic by Demeter.

TASTING ROOM INFORMATION: By appointment only

DIRECTIONS: From the intersection of Hwy 50 and Hwy 92 in Delta: Head east on Hwy 92 approximately 10 miles; turn left (north) onto Payne Siding Road (just past the town of Austin); turn right (east) onto North Road; turn left (north) to stay on North Road.

OTHER AMENITIES AT WINERY: N/A

WINE AVAILABLE FOR PURCHASE OUTSIDE OF WINERY: Yes

OTHER TASTING ROOM LOCATIONS: No

NOTES: ______________________________

____

____

____

LEROUX CREEK VINEYARDS

12388 3100 Road, Hotchkiss, CO 81419
970-872-4746
lerouxcreekinn.com
lerouxcreekinn@msn.com

OWNER: Yvon and Joanna

YEAR BEGAN OPERATION: 2005

AVERAGE CASES PRODUCED ANNUALLY: 600

WINES PRODUCED:
White: Cayuga White, Chambourcin
Red: Chambourcin, Merlot
Other: Rosé, Cherry wine and Port-style wine

MESSAGE FROM OWNER: Our vineyards cover four acres of our 54-acre farm. We grow two hybrid varieties—Chambourcin and Cayuga. All of our grapes are raised organically. The vineyard is in the West Elks AVA, and we share grapes, knowledge, experience and the occasional glass of wine with the other vintners in the area. We use local fruits when in season to make small quantities of delicious fruit wines.

Our grape harvest has become an annual event in our community, with folks from the surrounding area willing to help us when we pick our grapes. Everyone has a wonderful day with plenty of companionship, fresh air, fun, work, great food and a glass or two of current vintages. We certainly do appreciate their efforts that contribute so much to our harvest!

TASTING ROOM INFORMATION: Summer through fall, daily, from 11 a.m. to 5 p.m.

DIRECTIONS: From the intersection of Hwy 133 and Hwy 92 in Hotchkiss: Head west on Hwy 92; turn right (north) onto 3100 Road. The winery is approximately 2 miles down the road.

OTHER AMENITIES AT WINERY: Leroux Creek Inn & Vineyards Culinary Adventure stays; Wine experience featuring French-country gourmet lunch picnics and "Dining in the Vines" dinner series; Winery and vineyard tours, plus other fun activities; Leroux Creek Spa and products.

WINE AVAILABLE FOR PURCHASE OUTSIDE OF WINERY: Yes

OTHER TASTING ROOM LOCATIONS: No

NOTES: ____

____

____

____

MESA WINDS WINERY

31262 L Road, Hotchkiss, CO 81419
Mailing address: PO Box 327, Hotchkiss, CO 81419
970-250-4788
mesawindswinery.com
mail@mesawindsfarm.com

OWNER: Wink Davis and Max Eisele

YEAR BEGAN OPERATION: 2010

AVERAGE CASES PRODUCED ANNUALLY: 400

WINES PRODUCED:
White: Pinot Gris
Red: None
Other: Blend of Pinot Meunier/Pinot Noir; Rosé; Peach Fruit wine

MESSAGE FROM OWNER: Mesa Winds Farm & Winery is a diversified, family farm raising certified organic peaches, apples, cherries, wine grapes and table grapes as well as sheep. We craft our wines here on the farm using only our own fruit ("Estate Bottled") because we know that our grapes are raised with care, in healthy, living soils, and without the use of artificial chemicals and fertilizers. In our winery we let these grapes speak for themselves, expressing the true terroir and vintage variations expressive of our mountain valley. Our sheep mow and fertilize our orchards and vineyards for us to reduce the use of heavy equipment and fossil fuels.

Our Pinot Gris grapes yield a clean, dry, white wine with full-mouth feel and soft, lingering aftertastes. Pinot Meunier is a lesser-known varietal of the Pinot family, most commonly used for blending in Champagne. Our Meunier red wine and red blends are subtle, elegant, adventurous and feminine with a long finish and full-mouth feel.

In crafting our Rosé we blend our Meunier, Pinot Noir and Chambourçin grapes to produce a dry, light wine in the French café style, great for picnics or sipping on the patio. Our Peach wine brings back fond memories of the autumn peach harvest: slightly sweet and refreshing; it works marvelously as an aperitif or dessert wine.

TASTING ROOM INFORMATION: Memorial Day through October, Saturday and Sunday from 11 a.m. to 5 p.m.

DIRECTIONS: From Hotchkiss: Follow Hwy 92 to 3100 Road; turn right (north) onto 3100 Road; turn right (east) onto L Road (also called Ellington Road); the winery is ¼ mile on the right.

OTHER AMENITIES AT WINERY: Farm stay accommodations – see website for details.

WINE AVAILABLE FOR PURCHASE OUTSIDE OF WINERY: YES

OTHER TASTING ROOM LOCATIONS: No

NOTES: ____

____

____

MOUNTAIN VIEW WINERY

5859 58.25 Road, Olathe, CO 81425
970-323-6816
mountainviewwinery.com
mountainviewwinery@gmail.com

OWNER: Mike and Wendy Young

YEAR BEGAN OPERATION: 2000

AVERAGE CASES PRODUCED ANNUALLY: 1,000 - 3,000

WINES PRODUCED:
White: Chardonnay, Gewürztraminer, Pinot Grigio, Riesling
Red: Barbera, Merlot, Pinot Noir, Syrah
Other: Blends called: Dare Devil Red and Uncompahgre; Fruit wines, Port and Dessert wines

MESSAGE FROM OWNER: We are an orchard and a winery that have been in the family for over 50 years. Our goal is to take the hurry and hustle/bustle out of life for just a moment. We also sell "You-Pick" asparagus, apples, peaches, pears, plums and cherries in season. Come ready to sit and visit and enjoy!

TASTING ROOM INFORMATION: Monday through Saturday from 10 a.m. to 6 p.m. Our tasting room is open air, so come prepared in the winter months.

DIRECTIONS: From the intersection of Hwy 50 and Hwy 348 in Olathe: Head west on Hwy 348; turn right (north) onto 58.25 Road; the winery is at the first driveway on the left.

OTHER AMENITIES AT WINERY: We have indoor and outdoor options for hosting parties and events.

WINE AVAILABLE FOR PURCHASE OUTSIDE OF WINERY: Yes

OTHER TASTING ROOM LOCATIONS: Red Mountain Ranches, 19458 Hwy 65, Cedaredge, CO 81413 and West Fork Gallery, 105 S. 5th Street, Dolores, CO 81323

NOTES: ____

____

____

____

SNOW CAPPED CIDER

250 S. Grand Mesa Drive, Cedaredge, CO, 81413
970-856-7006
snowcappedcider.com
info.snowcappedcider@gmail.com

OWNER: Connie, Dan and Ty Williams

YEAR BEGAN OPERATION: 2013

AVERAGE CASES PRODUCED ANNUALLY: 800

WINES PRODUCED:
White: None
Red: None
Other: 6130' Dry, Boondocker Dry Hopped, Carmel Apple, Crabbly ol' Granny, Honey Crisp, Honey Crisp Ice, North 40, Poire Nouveau - Pear Cider, Sippin' Cider, Utopia

MESSAGE FROM OWNER: Our Snow Capped Ciders proudly follow in the great tradition of American hard cider makers. We are located in Cedaredge, Colorado - the heart of Colorado fruit growing country. The high altitude and cool nights produce some of the best apples in the country. Our ciders are made from freshly pressed apples grown in our own orchards. We never use juice concentrates and our ciders are naturally fermented. Our ciders have a fresh, clean taste with subtle undertones of various natural flavors.

Under the AppleShed family we also produce wines under the Williams Cellars label. In addition to our wines and ciders The AppleShed offers a unique shopping experience. Our Western art galleries are filled with paintings, photographs, pottery and sculptures from both local and regional artists. We provide an incredible shopping experience in our small boutique shops, which offer unique items perfect for your home and gifts for family and friends.

After tasting our wines and ciders and shopping at the various boutiques, stop for lunch at our Loading Dock Deli. Our menu serves good old fashioned food that is long on taste and short on cost. Come and give us a try!

TASTING ROOM INFORMATION: Monday through Saturday from 9 a.m. to 5 p.m., Sunday from 9 a.m. to 4 p.m.

DIRECTIONS: Located in The AppleShed on Hwy 65 (Grand Mesa Drive) in downtown Cedaredge.

OTHER AMENITIES AT WINERY: Numerous boutique shops selling a variety of merchandise; Western art in all media including painting, photography, sculpture and pottery; and The Loading Dock Deli. Facilities available for meetings and banquets.

WINE AVAILABLE FOR PURCHASE OUTSIDE OF WINERY: Yes

OTHER TASTING ROOM LOCATIONS: No

NOTES: ____

____

____

STONE COTTAGE CELLARS

41716 Reds Road, Paonia, CO 81428
970-527-3444
stonecottagecellars.com
info@stonecottagecellars.com

OWNER: Karen and Brent Helleckson

YEAR BEGAN OPERATION: 2003

AVERAGE CASES PRODUCED ANNUALLY: 650-800

WINES PRODUCED:
White: Chardonnay, Gewürztraminer, Pinot Gris
Red: Merlot, Pinot Noir, Syrah
Other: Alpine Dessert wine

MESSAGE FROM OWNER: We are a small, intimate estate winery reminiscent of Old Europe. The winery and outbuildings are constructed of local fieldstone, and the wines are crafted with similar attention to traditional quality.

TASTING ROOM INFORMATION: Memorial Day through October, daily, from 11 a.m. to 6 p.m.

DIRECTIONS: From the intersection of Hwy 187 and Hwy 133 near Paonia: Head north on Hwy 133; turn left (north) at the second left, which is Garvin Mesa Road; turn left (west) onto Recs Road.

OTHER AMENITIES AT WINERY: Vineyard tours, Cellar tours, vacation rental property on site - "The Stone Cottage" (sleeps 4).

WINE AVAILABLE FOR PURCHASE OUTSIDE OF WINERY: Yes

OTHER TASTING ROOM LOCATIONS: No

NOTES: ____

____

____

____

STONEY MESA WINERY

16199 Happy Hollow Road, Cedaredge, CO 81413
970-856-9463
stoneymesa.com
wine@stoneymesa.com

OWNER: Bret Neal

YEAR BEGAN OPERATION: 1990

AVERAGE CASES PRODUCED ANNUALLY: Information not Available

WINES PRODUCED:
White: Gewürztraminer, Pinot Gris, Riesling
Red: Cabernet Sauvignon, Merlot,
Other: Blend called Rojo del Mesa, Blush wine

MESSAGE FROM OWNER: Riesling is King at our modern facility, which utilizes proven Old World technology with modern equipment. We incorporate gentle fruit handling, temperature-controlled fermentation and small lot production into our wines.

Since starting in 1990, Stoney Mesa Winery has become a pioneer in the production of wine grapes and winemaking in Colorado. Our first vintage was released to the public in 1993 and, since then, we are highly regarded as one of the top white wine producers in the state.

Over the past 20 years, we have grown and expanded our facilities, production and vineyards but still focus on high quality wines at a great price. Stop by our winery or vineyard for tastings and tours.

TASTING ROOM INFORMATION: May through October, daily, from 11 a.m. to 5 p.m.; November through April, Monday through Saturday from 11 a.m. to 5 p.m., Sunday from noon to 3:30 p.m.

DIRECTIONS: From downtown Cedaredge on Hwy 65: Head south; turn right (west) onto SW 11th Avenue; turn left (south) onto Happy Hollow Road.

OTHER AMENITIES AT WINERY: Gift shop; available for event rental.

WINE AVAILABLE FOR PURCHASE OUTSIDE OF WINERY: Yes

OTHER TASTING ROOM LOCATIONS: No

NOTES: ____________________

____

____

____

TERROR CREEK WINERY

17445 Garvin Mesa Road, Paonia, CO 81428
970-527-3484
terrorcreekwinery.com
jmath@paonia.com

OWNER: John and Joan Mathewson

YEAR BEGAN OPERATION: 1992

AVERAGE CASES PRODUCED ANNUALLY: 500 - 800

WINES PRODUCED:
White: Unoaked Chardonnay, Gewürztraminer, Riesling
Red: Pinot Noir
Other: Blend called Chalet

MESSAGE FROM OWNER: John Mathewson, a Colorado School of Mines graduate, and his wife Joan, a Colorado Woman's College graduate, found this wonderful piece of land in the 1980s. They started planting vines next to a small plot of Gewürztraminer, which had been planted in 1972 as a part of Colorado State University's "Four Corners Project."

Today, the grapes are handpicked and crafted into wine by enologist, Joan, whose diploma was earned at "L'Ecole Changins" in Nyon, Switzerland. The wines are European in style - clean, fruity and true to the grape varietal...Delicious!

TASTING ROOM INFORMATION: Memorial Day weekend through September, daily, 11 a.m. to 5 p.m.; October, Saturday and Sunday from 11 a.m. to 5 p.m.

DIRECTIONS: From the intersection of Hwy 133 and Hwy 187 in Paonia: Head north on Hwy 133; turn left (north) onto Garvin Mesa Road. Winery is at the end of the road.

OTHER AMENITIES AT WINERY: Lovely gardens with magnificent views of the valley and West Elk Mountains.

WINE AVAILABLE FOR PURCHASE OUTSIDE OF WINERY: Yes

OTHER TASTING ROOM LOCATIONS: No

NOTES: ______________________________

____

____

____

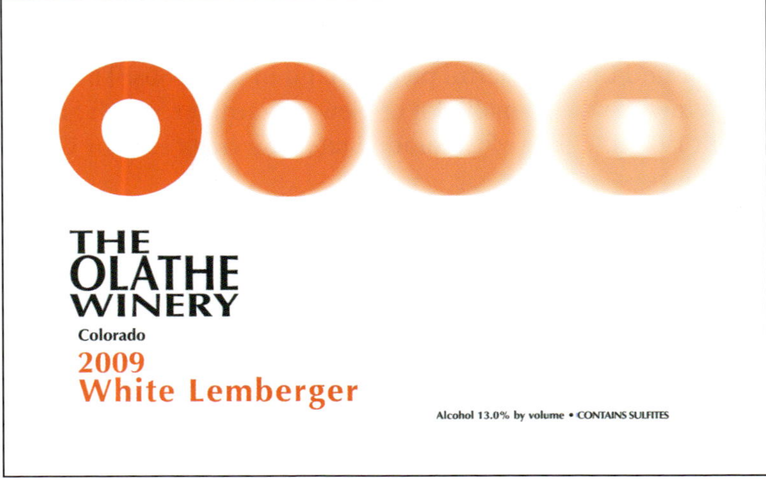

THE OLATHE WINERY

5482 Hwy 348, Olathe, CO 81425
Mailing address: PO Box 940, Olathe, CO 81425
970-323-6224
cottonwoodcellars.com
cowinelady@cs.com

OWNER: Keith and Diana Read

YEAR BEGAN OPERATION: 1994

AVERAGE CASES PRODUCED ANNUALLY: 3,500

WINES PRODUCED:
(Note: Not all wines are produced annually)
White: Chardonnay, White Pinot Noir
Red: Cabernet Franc, Cabernet Sauvignon, Reserve Cabernet Sauvignon, Lemberger, Merlot, Reserve Merlot, Pinot Noir, Syrah
Other: Blend called Classic Blend

MESSAGE FROM OWNER: Owner's Keith and Diana Read retired from the Tech industry in California and started the Cottonwood Cellars winery in 1994. Keith apprenticed to a chemist in winemaking, as well as developing an extensive library on Enology and Viticulture. They planted 22.5 acres in seven varieties from 1995 to 2000 at 5,400' altitude, from which they produce approximately 3,500 cases per year. The red wines and Chardonnay (Sur Lees) are aged in a combination of new and neutral oak barrels from nine months to two years. The wines have superior quality, being well-balanced and varietal correct.

TASTING ROOM INFORMATION: Memorial Day weekend through October, Wednesday through Saturday from 11 a.m. to 5:30 p.m.; April through Memorial Day and November through December, Friday and Saturday from 11 a.m. to 5 p.m. Closed January through March, except by appointment only.

DIRECTIONS: From the intersection of Hwy 50 and Hwy 348 in Olathe: Head west on Hwy 348. Winery is 3.4 miles on the right side.

OTHER AMENITIES AT WINERY: Event facilities in tasting room and barrel room (75 people), front lawn (125 sit down) or 300 people for weddings, receptions, reunions. We also sell gift items.

WINE AVAILABLE FOR PURCHASE OUTSIDE OF WINERY: Yes

OTHER TASTING ROOM LOCATIONS: Alpine Floral, 1414 Hawk Pkwy, Montrose, CO 81401 and The Designer's Vault, 214 8th Street #17, Glenwood Springs, CO 81601

NOTES: ____

____

____

____

WILLIAMS CELLARS

250 S. Grand Mesa Drive, Cedaredge, CO 81413
970-856-7006
theappleshed.net
info@theappleshed.net

OWNER: Connie, Dan and Ty Williams

YEAR BEGAN OPERATION: 2013

AVERAGE CASES PRODUCED ANNUALLY: 750

WINES PRODUCED:
White: Gewürztraminer, Moscato, Riesling
Red: Cabernet Sauvignon, Merlot, Pinot Noir, Tempranillo
Other: None

MESSAGE FROM OWNER: Williams Cellars is part of the AppleShed family. We have used our experience as four generations of fruit growers to produce some excellent wines. We also carry wines from other quality regional wineries. Our tasting room is located in the AppleShed and is open year-round. Come in and give us a taste. We think you will be pleasantly surprised with our wines!

In addition to Williams Cellars and Snow Capped Cider the AppleShed offers a unique shopping experience. Our Western art galleries are filled with paintings, photographs, pottery and sculptures from both local and regional artists. We provide an incredible shopping experience in our small boutique shops, which offer unique items perfect for your home and gifts for family and friends.

After tasting our wines and ciders and shopping at the various boutiques, stop for lunch at our Loading Dock Deli. Our menu serves good old fashioned food that is long on taste and short on cost. Come and give us a try!

TASTING ROOM INFORMATION: Monday through Saturday from 9 a.m. to 5 p.m., Sunday from 9 a.m. to 4 p.m.

DIRECTIONS: The winery is located in The AppleShed on Hwy 65 (Grand Mesa Drive) in downtown Cedaredge.

OTHER AMENITIES AT WINERY: Numerous boutique shops selling a variety of merchandise; Western art in all media including painting, photography, sculpture and pottery; and The Loading Dock Deli. Facilities available for meetings and banquets.

WINE AVAILABLE FOR PURCHASE OUTSIDE OF WINERY: Yes

OTHER TASTING ROOM LOCATIONS: No

NOTES: ______________________________

____

____

____

WOODY CREEK CELLARS

Mailing address: PO Box 69, Austin, CO 81410
970-901-7575
woodycreekcellars.com
Email: N/A

OWNER: Kevin Doyle

YEAR BEGAN OPERATION: 2000

AVERAGE CASES PRODUCED ANNUALLY: 2,000

WINES PRODUCED:
White: None
Red: Cabernet Franc, Cabernet Sauvignon, Grenache, Merlot, Pinot Noir, Sangiovese, Syrah, Tempranillo
Other: None

MESSAGE FROM OWNER: Woody Creek Cellars is dedicated to making fine natural wines with Old-World methods, using only Colorado's finest natural ingredients. We focus on small lot production and high quality. Guided by an ethos of simplicity, Woody Creek Cellars' handmade wines are made with primitive equipment.

Our focus is on new winery consultation, to help with solving problems with winemaking, assist new winery start-ups and to provide service to winery management.

Our wines are chemical-free, gravity flown, unfiltered and aged in French oak barrels. Woody Creek Cellars' wines are a benchmark for Colorado wines focusing on good quality at a great price. Our label features five interlocking hands, a symbol and reflection of owner/winemaker, Kevin Doyle's belief in a sense of community and strength through unity. When you stop by for a tasting, ask about our custom labeling on all of our wines!

TASTING ROOM INFORMATION: By appointment only

DIRECTIONS: Given at time of appointment reservation.

OTHER AMENITIES AT WINERY: N/A

WINE AVAILABLE FOR PURCHASE OUTSIDE OF WINERY: Yes

OTHER TASTING ROOM LOCATIONS: Palma Cigars, 2207 Larimer Street, Denver, CO 80205

NOTES: ____

____

____

____

WEST ELKS REGION

What Else To See & Do

Black Canyon of the Gunnison National National Park **nps.gov/blca/index.htm**
You take the South Rim and I'll take the North Rim, and both of us will see incredible sights! The park's many overlooks provide spectacular views of sheer, narrow canyon walls, which plummet to the Gunnison River. The roads can take you to several other recreation areas that border the park, and to the bottom of the canyon.

Curecanti National Recreation Area **nps.gov/cure/index.htm**
Fishing, boating, hiking, scenic drives…Curecanti Recreation Area has it all! Experience the panoramic mesas, fjord-like reservoirs and steep, narrow canyons. Three reservoirs make up this area: Crystal, Morrow Point and Blue Mesa. And, in case you need a little help catching a fish, Federal and State fish hatcheries stock them with over three million fish each year! The Elk Creek Visitor Center provides valuable information.

Delta - City of Murals **deltacountycolorado.com**
Pick up a brochure at the Delta Visitor Center, which will guide you to several buildings that depict local scenes painted by area artists.

Grand Mesa **grandmesabyway.com**
Ever been on the world's largest flat-top mountain? Grand Mesa offers a variety of outdoor activities ranging from sightseeing, hiking, biking and fishing during the summer and fall. In the winter, the activities include cross-country skiing, snowshoeing and snowmobiling. **Powderhorn Mountain Resort** offers downhill skiing and summer activities (**www.powderhorn.com**). A 63-mile drive takes you over the Mesa from Delta and Montrose Counties into the Grand Valley, offering numerous scenic stops along the way.

Museum of the Mountain West **museumofthemountainwest.org**
This gem of a museum has tons of western memorabilia primarily collected by Richard Fike, a retired historical archaeologist and author. This is a step back in time with your own tour guide making history come alive for all ages.

Morrow Point Boat Tours **nps.gov/cure/planyourvisit/boattour.htm**
Travel into the Black Canyon of the Gunnison via a boat tour led by a park ranger. Learn about the geology, the dams and reservoirs and the wildlife.

Outdoor Activities
Outdoor activities abound throughout this area every season of the year.

- **Fishing** **nps.gov/cure/index.htm & visitmontrose.com**
- **Hiking, Biking** **trails.com & numerous websites**
- **Rafting** **visitmontrose.com**
- **Winter Activities** **visitmontrose.com**

Pioneer Town **pioneertown.org**
What was life like in the late 1800s in Cedaredge, Colorado? Experience a bygone era at this reconstructed town where all the structures are either original restorations or authentic replicas. Over 20 buildings line the boardwalk and are packed with history.

The Creamery Arts Center **creameryartscenter.org**
What does cream have to do with art? The 1930's Creamery Building has been renovated, and is now a cooperative featuring 60 area artists. Their work is displayed in a dramatic two-story gallery. They host a monthly Artist Reception with art, food, wine and beer. And they even serve ice cream!

West Elk Scenic By-Way **westelkbyway.com**
The By-Way provides 204-miles of incredible scenery, history of Western Colorado and a winery or two along the way! This roadway passes through rural, designated Wilderness and National Forests, providing you with potential glimpses of animals and wildflowers along the way.

For further information, please visit these websites:

cedaredgecolorado.com **co.montrose.co.us**
deltacolorado.org **deltacountycolorado.com**
hotchkisschamber.com **paoniachamber.com**
visitmontrose.com

NOTES:

Four Corners Region

Wine Fact

In ancient Greece, a dinner host would take the first sip of wine to assure guests the wine was not poisoned, hence the phrase "drinking to one's health." "Toasting" started in ancient Rome when the Romans continued the Greek tradition but started dropping a piece of toasted bread into each wine glass to temper undesirable tastes or excessive acidity.

http://facts.randomhistory.com/2009/08/21_wine.html

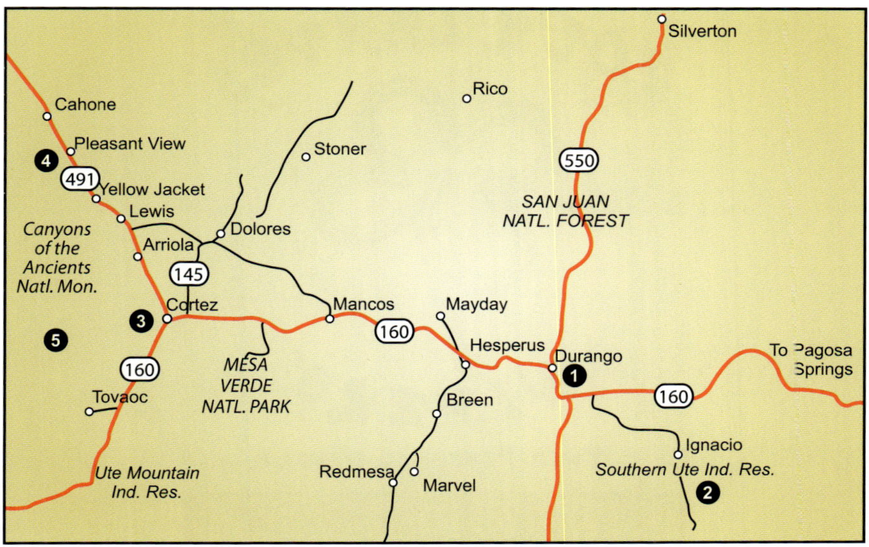

Four Corners Region Wineries

1. Four Leaves Winery
2. Fox Fire Farms
3. Guy Drew Vineyards
4. Pleasant View Winery
5. Sutcliffe Vineyards

FOUR LEAVES WINERY

528 Main Avenue, Durango, CO 81301
970-403-8182
fourleaveswinery.com
info@fourleaveswinery.com

OWNER: Dean Fagner

YEAR BEGAN OPERATION: 2011

AVERAGE CASES PRODUCED ANNUALLY: Information not Available

WINES PRODUCED:
White: Chardonnay, Pinot Grigio, Reisling, Viognier
Red: Barbera, Malbec, Pinot Noir, Sangiovese, Tempranillo
Other: Numerous red blends, Fruit wines, Port wines, Ice wine

MESSAGE FROM OWNER: Four Leaves Winery is a boutique winery located in downtown Durango. We import the highest quality grapes and then handcraft, blend and ferment all of our wines right in front of you! Want to create a custom blend that is all your own? Our staff can guide you through making your very own wine! In addition to having a custom blend, you can enjoy a bottling party with friends, and each bottle will have your own personalized label.

We are located right across the street from the Durango & Silverton Railroad Depot in downtown Durango. Drop in and enjoy a wine tasting, a glass of wine, or pick up a bottle before or after your train ride!

TASTING ROOM INFORMATION: Monday through Saturday from noon to 8 p.m., Sunday from noon to 7 p.m.

DIRECTIONS: Located in downtown Durango, across the street from the Durango & Silverton Narrow Gauge Railroad Depot.

OTHER AMENITIES AT WINERY: Wine-related merchandise and light appetizers. We are available for private parties, events and weddings. Art work is available for purchase. We allow our customers to make their own wine and bottle it when it is ready.

WINE AVAILABLE FOR PURCHASE OUTSIDE OF WINERY: Yes

OTHER TASTING ROOM LOCATIONS: No

NOTES: ______________________________

____

____

____

FOX FIRE FARMS

5513 County Road 321, Ignacio, CO 81137
970-563-4675
foxfirefarms.com
info@foxfirefarms.com

OWNER: Richard and Linda Parry

YEAR BEGAN OPERATION: 2009

AVERAGE CASES PRODUCED ANNUALLY: 600

WINES PRODUCED:
White: Brianna, Chardonnay, Riesling, Traminette
Red: Cabernet Sauvignon, Corot Noir, Marquette, Merlot, Pinot Noir
Other: Fox Fire Red, Mandarin Orange Muscat, Pomegranate and Strawberry Fruit wines

MESSAGE FROM OWNER: Fox Fire Farms is Southwest Colorado's premier vineyard and winery, with a long history of being the Southwest's premier organic livestock farm. The livestock farm has been in continuous operation for 100 years with 5 generations living and working on the farm. Located 20 miles southeast of Durango and 30 miles southwest of Pagosa Springs as part of a 1,000 acre farm in a stunning Colorado setting. We have developed a local and national reputation as practitioners of sustainable agriculture.

A few years ago we branched out into viticulture and have begun producing delicious wine. In addition to the noble grape varieties of wine, we are now producing cold-weather hybrid wines that you will not find anywhere else in Colorado. Please stop by!

TASTING ROOM INFORMATION: May 15 through October 31. Thursday through Sunday from 1 to 6 p.m. Off-season by appointment only.

DIRECTIONS: From downtown Ignacio: Head east on Hwy 151; turn right (south) onto Hwy 321. We are 4 miles from the intersection of Hwy 151 and Hwy 321.

OTHER AMENITIES AT WINERY: Wine-related merchandise. We are available for private parties, events, meetings and weddings, all of which can be catered. We also have overnight parking for "Harvest Host" members.

WINE AVAILABLE FOR PURCHASE OUTSIDE OF WINERY: Yes

OTHER TASTING ROOM LOCATIONS: See website for yearly roster of satellite tasting rooms.

NOTES: ______________________________________

____

____

____

GUY DREW VINEYARDS

19891 Road G, Cortez, CO 81321
Mailing address: PO Box 1750, Cortez, CO 81321
970-565-9211
guydrewvineyards.com
guydrew@q.com

OWNER: Guy and Ruth Drew

YEAR BEGAN OPERATION: 2000

AVERAGE CASES PRODUCED ANNUALLY: 3,500

WINES PRODUCED:
White: Unoaked Chardonnay, Gewürztraminer, Riesling, Viognier
Red: Baco Noir, Cabernet Sauvignon, Merlot, Syrah
Other: Meritage, Port wine

MESSAGE FROM OWNER: We focus on fruit grown in Colorado. We have Estate vineyards and purchase from six growers in the Four Corners area that grow for us. We also source fruit from Palisade, primarily from Talbott Farms. Our state-of-the-art winemaking facility allows us to make premium Colorado wines at reasonable prices. We have won many awards from international wine competitions and have had accolades from national media.

The Four Corners region and Montezuma County have incredible potential for growing premium wine grapes. There are vineyards from just over 5,000' up to 7,000' in elevation that give us diverse growing micro-climates, and creates the opportunity to grow many different varieties.

TASTING ROOM INFORMATION: Daily, from noon to 5 p.m.

DIRECTIONS: From downtown Cortez: Head south on Hwy 160/491; turn right (west) onto Road G; the winery is 4 miles down the road.

OTHER AMENITIES AT WINERY: Bistro tables in our courtyard (bring your own food)

WINE AVAILABLE FOR PURCHASE OUTSIDE OF WINERY: Yes

OTHER TASTING ROOM LOCATIONS: Ute Mountain Indian Trading Company & Gallery, 27601 E. Hwy 160, Cortez, CO 81321

NOTES: ______________________________

____

____

____

PLEASANT VIEW VINEYARDS

22970 County Road 10, Pleasant View, CO 81331
Mailing address: PO Box 249, Pleasant View, CO 81331
970-562-6372
pleasantviewvineyards.info
pvvineyards@fone.net

OWNER: Elizabeth and Allan Bleak

YEAR BEGAN OPERATION: 2011

AVERAGE CASES PRODUCED ANNUALLY: 100

WINES PRODUCED:
White: Chardonnay
Red: Pinot Noir
Other: None

MESSAGE FROM OWNER: Elizabeth and Allan Bleak started building their home in Pleasant View, Colorado in 1997 and became residents in 2000. The vineyard and orchard were established in 2001, with the help of their family and friends. Many years of thoughtful trial and error and perseverance have culminated into a love of viticulture, and naturally the end product, wine. We hope you enjoy our wines as much as we have enjoyed and loved our journey to bring them to you!

Pleasant View Vineyards, is nestled among old-growth juniper and pinion forests adjacent to the Canyons of the Ancients. This Single Vineyard Canyon Country wine truly has captured the same delicate, yet very robust, essence that is experienced when visiting the surrounding Canyons and National Monuments. Our organic growing practices have been maintained since the initial planting in 2001, and we do not use any chemicals. We conserve water, utilizing a drip irrigation system, and in keeping with sustainability and ecological considerations, all water and pressed grape skins are worked back into the soil from which they came.

TASTING ROOM INFORMATION: By appointment only

DIRECTIONS: From the intersection of Hwy 184 and Hwy 491 north of Cortez: Head north on Hwy 491; turn left (west) at MM45 onto BB Road; turn left (south) onto County Road 10 (approximately 5 miles). The winery is 3 miles down the road on left (white gates, red flowers on gates).

OTHER AMENITIES AT WINERY: N/A

WINE AVAILABLE FOR PURCHASE OUTSIDE OF WINERY: Yes

OTHER TASTING ROOM LOCATIONS: No

NOTES: ______________________________

____

____

____

SUTCLIFFE VINEYARDS

12174 Road G, Cortez, CO 81321
970-565-0825
sutcliffewines.com
info@sutcliffewines.com

OWNER: John Sutcliffe

YEAR BEGAN OPERATION: 1999

AVERAGE CASES PRODUCED ANNUALLY: 4,000

WINES PRODUCED:
White: Chardonnay, Riesling, Sauvignon Blanc, Viognier
Red: Cabernet Franc, Cabernet Sauvignon, Cinsaut, Merlot, Petit Verdot, Syrah
Other: Blends called Beddgelert, Down Caynon, Field Blend, Tierra del Fuego,Trawsfynydd; Doce Pecado and Nectar dessert wines

MESSAGE FROM OWNER: The first vines were planted in 1995 on the architect's aesthetic whim, with no lofty dream of having a vineyard. The first harvest was in 1999, and the wines produced were marketed in 2001. They were small bottlings of Merlot, Cabernet Franc and Syrah.

Our current winemaker, Joe Buckel, joined us from the Sonoma Valley after a career with BR Cohn, Flowers and Rutz. He loves the wines of Burgundy and the Rhone, and he exercises both restraint and patience in making his elegant wines. We are invariably told that our wines have an Old World style.

As an ex-restaurateur, John Sutcliffe from the very start was most comfortable selling to restaurants, and our penetration of that market in Aspen, Telluride, Vail, New York and restaurants on the West Coast was new for Colorado wines. We also raise livestock, cut hay and grow orchard fruit as well as grapes.

TASTING ROOM INFORMATION: Daily, from 11 a.m. to 5 p.m.

DIRECTIONS: From the intersection of Hwy 491 and Hwy 160 in Cortez: Head south on Hwy 419/160; turn right (west) onto Road G/County Road G at the Cortez Municipal Airport; the winery is approximately 13 miles down the road.

OTHER AMENITIES AT WINERY: Annual harvest dinner at our farm at Dunton Hot Springs in Dolores; a variety of events; we are a working farm.

WINE AVAILABLE FOR PURCHASE OUTSIDE OF WINERY: Yes

OTHER TASTING ROOM LOCATIONS: No

NOTES: ______________________________

____

____

____

FOUR CORNERS REGION

What Else To See & Do

Archeological Sites **see Tourism & Chamber of Commerce websites below**

Want to know what the Ancestral Pueblo people used a kiva for? The Four Corners region of southwest Colorado is an archaeological Mecca! Here you can visit numerous ruins, with major sites located at Mesa Verde, Hovenweep and Ute Mountain Tribal Park.

- **Mesa Verde National Park** **nps.gov/meve**
  Visit some of the most well-preserved archeological sites in the United States and learn about the people who lived there for over 700 years. Experience breathtaking vistas on your scenic drive or partake in self-guided and ranger-led tours through many of the cliff dwellings.

- **Hovenweep** **nps.gov/hove**
  Walk among multi-storied towers at this Monument that protects six prehistoric, Puebloan-era villages that were occupied from approximately 500 to 1300 AD. Square Tower offers a Visitor Center and interpretive trail.

- **Ute Mountain Tribal Park** **utemountaintribalpark.info**
  Take a guided tour with a Ute tribal member, visit an ancestral pueblo and see petroglyphs and artifacts at this fascinating site.

Durango & Silverton Narrow Gauge Railroad **durangotrain.com**
Take a ride on this historic train through spectacular scenery, traveling round-trip from Durango to Silverton. The vintage, steam locomotive train operates year-round. Advance reservations are highly recommended.

Four Corners **navajonationparks.org/htm/fourcorners/htm**
Here is your chance to stand in four states at the same time: Colorado, New Mexico, Arizona and Utah! Nowhere else in the United States can you experience this.

Gambling **skyutecasino.com**
Try your luck at the Sky Ute Casino located on the Southern Ute Indian Reservation near Ignacio.

Highway 550 - San Juan Skyway & Million Dollar Highway
Fasten your seat belts and get your camera ready, as this spectacular drive with its breathtaking views takes you from the Four Corners area into other southwest Colorado towns such as Silverton, Ouray, Ridgeway and Telluride.

Hot Springs see information in **Mountain Region** section

Outdoor Activities - An adventure awaits you!

- **Hiking and Biking** **trails.com**
  Like anywhere in Colorado, the Four Corners region offers numerous hiking and biking trails. Detailed information is available at this and other websites.

- **Horseback Riding** **see websites below**
  "Saddle Up!" There are numerous stables in the area offering horseback riding excursions.

- **Rafting** **see websites below**
  Put on your helmet, PFD, and prepare to get wet. Numerous companies offer guided raft trips down the Animas River.

- **Vallecito Lake** **vallecitolakechamber.com**
  From fishing to snowshoeing to the Tour of Carvings, this beautiful lake offers numerous, year-round outdoor activities.

Purgatory Resort **purgatoryresort.com**
Take in the magnificent views of the San Juan Mountains while enjoying winter or summer activities at Purgatory Resort. During the winter months, ski on some of the 85 downhill trails or enjoy dog sledding, snowcat trips, snowmobiling, cross-country skiing and sleigh rides. During the summer, take a scenic chairlift ride, go horseback riding, hiking or mountain biking, or experience the thrill of a zipline.

For further information, please visit these websites:
durango.org **cortezchamber.com** **doloreschamber.com**
ignaciochamber.org **co.laplata.co.us/visitors**

NOTES:

Front Range Region

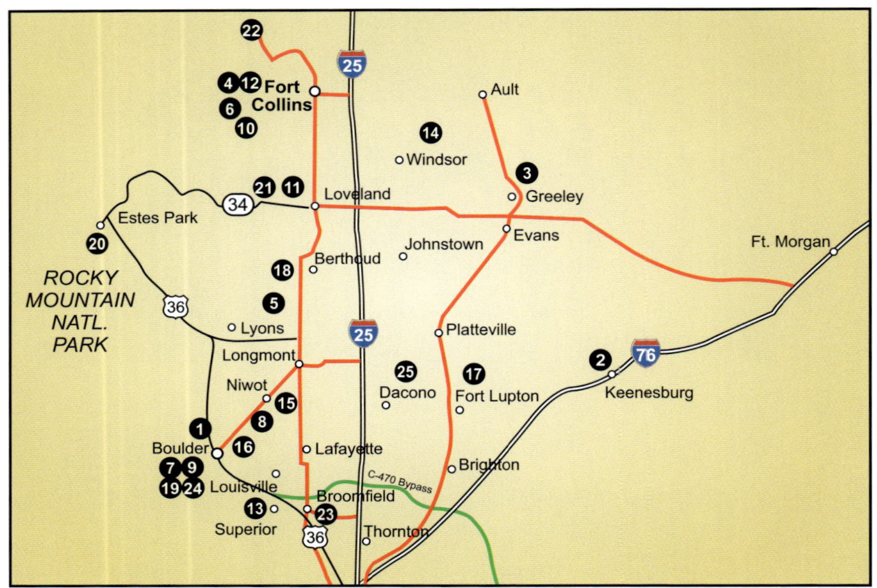

Front Range Region Wineries - North

1. Augustina's Winery
2. Bad Bitch Cellars
3. Bijou Creek Vineyards
4. Blossomwood Cidery
5. Blue Mountain Vineyards
6. Blue Skies Winery
7. Bookcliff Vineyards
8. Boulder Creek Winery
9. Boulder Wine Studios
10. Branch Out Cider
11. Climb Hard Cider
12. Compass Cider
13. HoneyJack Meadery
14. Hunters Moon Meadery
15. Medovina
16. Redstone Meadery
17. River Garden Winery
18. St. Vrain Vineyards & Winery
19. Settembre Cellars
20. Snowy Peaks Winery
21. Sweetheart City Winery
22. Ten Bears Winery
23. Turquoise Mesa Winery
24. What We Love, the winery
25. Wild Cider

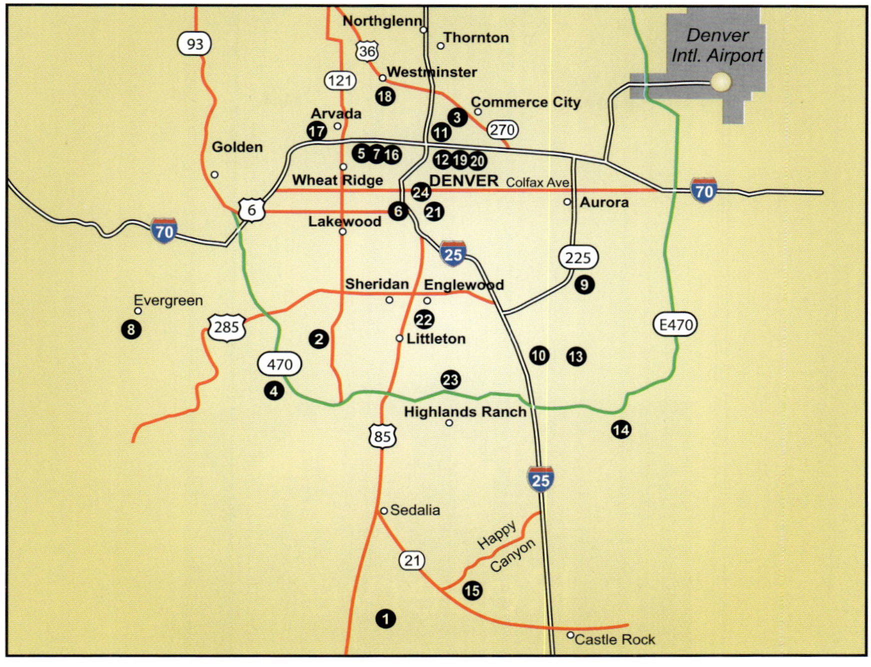

Front Range Region Wineries - South

1. Allis Ranch Winery
2. Avanti Winery
3. Balistreri Vineyards
4. Black Arts Cellars
5. Bonacquisti Wine Company
6. Colorado Cider Company
7. Colorado Winery Row
8. Creekside Cellars
9. Dragon Meadery
10. InVINtions Winery
11. Kingman Estates Winery
12. Mile High Winery
13. Point Blank Winery
14. Purgatory Cellars
15. Ruby Trust Cellars
16. Ryker's Cellars
17. Silver Vines Winery
18. Spero Winery
19. Stem Ciders
20. The Infinite Monkey Theorem
21. Verso Cellars
22. Waters Edge Winery
23. Water2Wine
24. Wild Women Wine

ALLIS RANCH WINERY

901 Allis Ranch Road, Sedalia, CO 80135
303-881-1294
allisranchwine.com
allisranchwine@gmail.com

OWNER: David Rhyne

YEAR BEGAN OPERATION: 2007

AVERAGE CASES PRODUCED ANNUALLY: 400-500

WINES PRODUCED:
White: Roussanne, Viognier
Red: Grenache, Reserve Syrah, Two Husky Syrah
Other: Rosé

MESSAGE FROM OWNER: Allis Ranch Winery is a family-owned, boutique winery near Sedalia, Colorado. We focus on Rhone varietals using small-lot vinification to create focused, handcrafted wines. All grapes are sourced from top growers on the Western Slope of Colorado. Allis Ranch Winery uses sustainable practices throughout the operation by minimizing the use of water and energy wherever possible.

After a great deal of research and samplings of Colorado wines, we determined that the Western Slope area offers a climate and altitude that would highlight the qualities of the grapes which originated in the Southern Rhone area of France. The hot days and cool nights bring out the classic fruit and black pepper of Syrah and the melon, floral and citric character in Viognier. Co-fermenting the Viognier grape with the Syrah, adds depth and structure to the Syrah.

TASTING ROOM INFORMATION: By appointment only

DIRECTIONS: From I-25 and Exit #182 (Wilcox Wolfensberger Road in Castle Rock): Head west on Wolfensberger Road; turn left (south) onto Hwy 105 (Perry Park Road); at 1.3 miles turn right (west) onto Allis Ranch Road.

OTHER AMENITIES AT WINERY: N/A

WINE AVAILABLE FOR PURCHASE OUTSIDE OF WINERY: Yes

OTHER TASTING ROOM LOCATIONS: No

NOTES: ____________________

____

____

____

AUGUSTINA'S WINERY

4715 N. Broadway B-3, Boulder, CO 80304
303-545-2047
winechick.biz
winechic@boulder.net

OWNER: Marianne "Gussie" Walter

YEAR BEGAN OPERATION: 1997

AVERAGE CASES PRODUCED ANNUALLY: 600

WINES PRODUCED:
White: Sauvignon Blanc, Vignoles
Red: Cabernet Franc, Merlot, Pinot Noir, Shiraz,
Other: Blends called Bottoms Up Red, Boulder Porch White, Marechal Foch, WineChick White, WineChick Cherry, Venus de Vino Rosé

MESSAGE FROM OWNER: Augustina's Winery is the oldest winery in Boulder County. It is the only one-woman winery in Colorado. I use only Colorado-grown grapes to make wines, which go with backpacking adventures, poker parties, good books or trashy novels and gingersnaps.

TASTING ROOM INFORMATION: April through November, Wednesdays and Saturdays (call ahead for hours). June through September, Fridays at the Boulder Farmers Market.

DIRECTIONS: From downtown Boulder: Head north on Broadway about 3.5 miles; turn left (west) at 4715 N. Broadway (by seasonal greenhouse/nursery). Behind the nursery is a warehouse building. The winery is on the south side - #B3.

OTHER AMENITIES AT WINERY: N/A

WINE AVAILABLE FOR PURCHASE OUTSIDE OF WINERY: Yes

OTHER TASTING ROOM LOCATIONS: Boulder Farmers Market, 13th Street between Canyon and Arapahoe, Boulder, CO 80302 and Dillon Farmers Market, Buffalo Street, Dillon, CO 80435

NOTES: ____

____

____

____

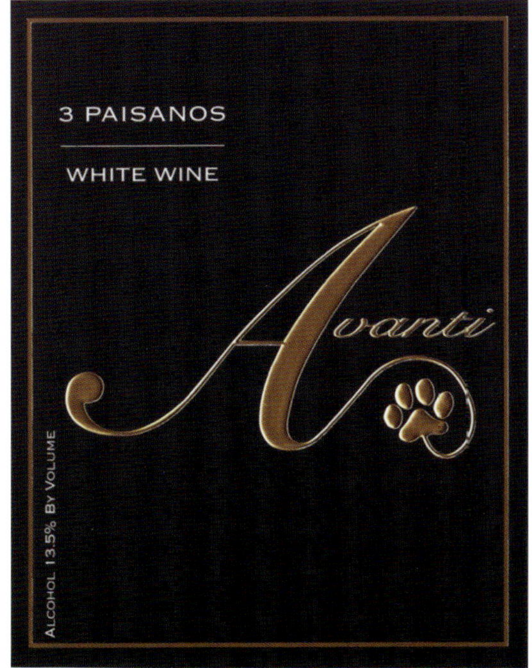

AVANTI WINERY

9046 W. Bowles Avenue, Littleton, CO 80123
303-904-7650
avantiwinery.com
grifgarman@aol.com

OWNER: Jim "Griff" Griffin

YEAR BEGAN OPERATION: 1997

AVERAGE CASES PRODUCED ANNUALLY: Information not Available

WINES PRODUCED:
White: Chardonnay
Red: Reserve Cabernet Sauvignon, Reserve Merlot
Other: Blends called 3 Paisanos White Table Wine, DueAmori, Grassetto Rosso, Bambino Tuscano, Niko's Classico, Three Amigos, Mystique, Port III

MESSAGE FROM OWNER: Avanti Winery was actually started as a way to promote other Colorado wineries. Currently we offer a variety of wines from over 20 different wineries. Please see our website for a complete listing. Our Avanti wines are a unique blend of the finest grapes grown. We have a sommelier on staff to assist with the blending, to insure the highest quality wines possible.

Owner "Griff" Griffin, who has lived in Colorado since 1971, and his wife, Jan, a Denver native, enjoy sharing their Colorado knowledge and can assist you in organizing your itinerary as you travel around Colorado's scenic by-ways. Stop by the winery for information as well as sampling!

TASTING ROOM INFORMATION: Thursday through Saturday from 10 a.m. to 6 p.m., Sunday from 11 a.m. to 4 p.m.

DIRECTIONS: From the intersection of Wadsworth Boulevard and Bowles Avenue in Littleton: Head west on Bowles Avenue. The winery is located on the south side of Southwest Plaza, between Guirys and Carpet Mill.

OTHER AMENITIES AT WINERY: A walk-in humidor featuring all major cigar brands (non-smoking facility)

WINE AVAILABLE FOR PURCHASE OUTSIDE OF WINERY: Yes

OTHER TASTING ROOM LOCATIONS: No

NOTES: ____

____

____

____

BBC WINES / BAD BITCH CELLARS

Hwy 4 and Hwy 53, Hudson, CO 80642
Mailing address; P.O. Box 146, Henderson, CO 80640
303-807-3906
badbitchcellars.com and eventswine.com
cellardog07@gmail.com

OWNER: Teresa Kernan

YEAR BEGAN OPERATION: 2012

AVERAGE CASES PRODUCED ANNUALLY: 250

WINES PRODUCED:
White: Numerous white wines
Red: Numerous red wines
Other: Numerous blends

MESSAGE FROM OWNER: Bad Bitch Cellars was created all because two girls loved to go to wine tastings and the adventure of traveling the world in search of their next favorite wine. These two girls are not afraid of entrepreneurship and the history of wine is fascinating to them.

On a special day in 2008, a daughter of one of the owners was to be wed. This daughter, like every bride had a vision and a budget, so we created her very own special wine. The response from family and special friends was so complimentary. Over time we have expanded from just "wedding wines" and the scope of creating wine for your special event is endless. We know people have a tremendous amount of planning and organizing for their special day or event, so let us take care of the wine!

TASTING ROOM INFORMATION: By appointment only

DIRECTIONS: Located by the Animal Sanctuary in Keenesburg; call for specific directions

OTHER AMENITIES AT WINERY: Wine-related merchandise

WINE AVAILABLE FOR PURCHASE OUTSIDE OF WINERY: Yes

OTHER TASTING ROOM LOCATIONS: By appointment at the Noah's Event Center, 11885 N. Bradburn Blvd. Westminster, CO 80031

NOTES: ______________________________

____

____

____

BALISTRERI VINEYARDS

1946 E. 66th Avenue, Denver, CO 80229
303-287-5156
balistrerivinewine.com
info@balistreriwine.com

OWNER: John, Birdie and Julie Balistreri

YEAR BEGAN OPERATION: 1998

AVERAGE CASES PRODUCED ANNUALLY: 5,000

WINES PRODUCED:
White: Chardonnay, dry Muscat, Viognier
Red: Cabernet Franc, Cabernet Sauvignon, Merlot, Petit Sirah, Sangiovese, Syrah, Tempranillo, Zinfandel
Other: Dessert wines

MESSAGE FROM OWNER: Balistreri Vineyards is a family-owned and operated winery dedicated to making fine-quality wine. John Balistreri's wines are made completely natural, with a very approachable, easy-drinking style. He combines both traditional winemaking methods and modern technology to produce award-winning wines. The wines are handcrafted one barrel at a time, with grapes that are fermented on their own yeast, unaltered by sulfates, unfiltered, unfined and aged in American oak.

TASTING ROOM INFORMATION: Daily, from 11 a.m. to 5 p.m.

DIRECTIONS: From the intersection of I-25 and 58th Avenue: Head east on 58th Avenue; turn left (north) onto Washington Street; turn right (east) onto 66th Street; the winery is on the south side of the street. Also accessible off I-270 and York Street exit.

OTHER AMENITIES AT WINERY: Complimentary tastings of our wines and tour of our wine cellar and winemaking facilities. Wine-related merchandise and gift baskets. Enjoy lunch or order small plates from our lunch menu during business hours. The Winery & Event Center is available for private parties and events after hours.

WINE AVAILABLE FOR PURCHASE OUTSIDE OF WINERY: Yes

OTHER TASTING ROOM LOCATIONS: No

NOTES: ______________________________

____

____

____

BIJOU CREEK VINEYARDS

2525 West 10th Street, Greeley, CO 80634
970-381-5614
bijoucreekwine.com
ewhillmann@earthlink.net

OWNER: Erwin Hillmann

YEAR BEGAN OPERATION: 2006

AVERAGE CASES PRODUCED ANNUALLY: 300

WINES PRODUCED:
White: Chardonnay, Riesling
Red: Cabernet Franc, Merlot, Syrah
Other: None

MESSAGE FROM OWNER: Born out of my love of fine wines, Bijou Creek Winery was started in Fort Morgan, Colorado as a part-time endeavor while I was still working a full time job. In 2014 Bijou Creek relocated to our current location at 2525 West 10th Street in Greeley, Colorado to expand production and open a tasting room. Please see our website for current tasting room hours.

My biggest challenge has been finding the right, high-quality Colorado grapes in sufficient quantities to meet our needs. Because of some recent challenging weather conditions in Colorado causing local grape shortages, we now also source grapes from other locations including prime vineyards in Washington, New Mexico and California. We are dedicated to offering only the finest wine made from premium grapes of several varieties from both red and white grapes. See our website for wine selection and price. Come and taste the experience for yourself!

TASTING ROOM INFORMATION: See website

DIRECTIONS: From I-25 and Exit #257: Head east on Hwy 34; turn left (north) onto Hwy 34 – Business (W. 10th Street); the winery is just past 26th Avenue.

OTHER AMENITIES AT WINERY: N/A

WINE AVAILABLE FOR PURCHASE OUTSIDE OF WINERY: Yes

OTHER TASTING ROOM LOCATIONS: Highlands Ranch Farmers Market, 9288 Dorchester Street, Highlands Ranch, CO 80129

NOTES: ____

____

____

____

BLACK ARTS CELLARS
11616 Shaffer Place #S-110, Littleton, CO 80127
303-722-0669
bacellars.com
info@bacellars.com

OWNER: John and Liz Cowperthwaite

YEAR BEGAN OPERATION: 2014

AVERAGE CASES PRODUCED ANNUALLY: ≤1000

WINES PRODUCED:
White: Sauvignon Blanc
Red: Cabernet Franc, Grenache, Petite Sirah, Syrah
Other: Rhône style white and red blends; Rosé

MESSAGE FROM OWNER: John and Liz started making wine in 2008 after visiting the Margaret River wine region of Western Australia. John pursued a 2-year degree in Oenology from the University of California—Davis to help find answers to "how great wine is made." At UC Davis, his PhD mentors revealed that despite advances in biochemistry and microbiology, a bit of the unknown still factors into the making of exceptional wines.

The name Black Arts Cellars is a nod to this component of mystery in winemaking. It is also a homage to Renaissance tarot and the art of fortune telling. Black Arts Cellars is a craft, urban winery, with a focus on the Rhône varietals. We import our grapes from the Central Coast of California, the Pacific Northwest and the Colorado Grand Valley. Roussanne and Viognier are our whites, made annually, with Grenache Noir, Mourvèdre, Petit Sirah and Syrah representing our reds. We also make a small-lot pink "GSM" in the spring, as well as small lots of Sauvignon Blanc and Cabernet Franc.

TASTING ROOM INFORMATION: May through mid-September, most Fridays from 3 to 7 p.m., Saturday and Sunday from noon to 6 p.m.; other times by appointment only.

DIRECTIONS: From C-470 and W. Ken Caryl Avenue: Head east on W. Ken Caryl Avenue; turn right (south) onto Simms Street (also called Chatfield Avenue); turn right (west) onto Shaffer Place; the winery will be on your left.

OTHER AMENITIES AT WINERY: No

WINE AVAILABLE FOR PURCHASE OUTSIDE OF WINERY: No

OTHER TASTING ROOM LOCATIONS: No

NOTES: ____

BLOSSOMWOOD CIDERY, LLC

216 N. College Avenue, Fort Collins, CO 80524
970-372-1350
compasscider.com
needle@compasscider.com

OWNER: Compass Cider House, Inc.

YEAR BEGAN OPERATION: 2005

AVERAGE CASES PRODUCED ANNUALLY: 3,000

WINES PRODUCED:
White: None
Red: None
Other: Hard Ciders and Perry

MESSAGE FROM OWNER: Blossomwood Cidery is the oldest cidery in the Rocky Mountains. We specialize in premium, artisan European-Style Ciders and Perry. We make our Ciders and Perry from a variety of fruit grown on the Western Slope of Colorado, with much of it fermented and aged in oak barrels.

TASTING ROOM INFORMATION: Located at Compass Cider House, 216 N. College Avenue, Fort Collins, CO 80524. Tuesday through Thursday from 4 to 10 p.m., Friday and Saturday from noon to 10 p.m., Sunday noon to 7 p.m.

DIRECTIONS: From I-25 and Exit #269B: Head west on Hwy 14 (Mulberry Street); turn right (north) onto College Avenue; the cidery is on your right in historic downtown Ft. Collins.

OTHER AMENITIES AT WINERY: Full kitchen with daily lunch and pairing menu. Private parties and events also hosted. Live music weekly.

WINE AVAILABLE FOR PURCHASE OUTSIDE OF WINERY: Yes

OTHER TASTING ROOM LOCATIONS: No

NOTES: ____

____

____

____

BLUE MOUNTAIN VINEYARDS

4480 Hoot Owl Drive, Berthoud, CO 80513
303-532-6104
coloradobluemountain.com
bill@coloradobluemountain.com

OWNER: Bill Prewitt

YEAR BEGAN OPERATION: 2007

AVERAGE CASES PRODUCED ANNUALLY: Information not Available

WINES PRODUCED:
White: Chardonnay, Gewürztraminer, Pinot Grigio, Riesling, Sauvignon Blanc
Red: Cabernet Sauvignon, Merlot, Malbec, Pinot Noir, Sangiovese, Zinfandel
Other: Golden Harvest

MESSAGE FROM OWNER: Our vineyard, winery and grounds are all built on the edge of a lake, with breathtaking scenery. Owner, Bill Prewitt has been making wine for over 42 years. Our vineyard and winery are family owned, like most in Colorado, and we want to make a nice wine that our customers can depend on for quality. Our wines are deep and rich for the reds, and wonderful and fruity for the whites. Malbec, Pinot Noir, Riesling and Zinfandel are our best sellers. We really encourage all of our customers to taste our wines before they buy them, to make sure they meet their taste profile. If you cannot travel to our Tasting Room, the wines are also available at liquor stores in Denver, Estes Park, Fort Collins, Greeley, Longmont and Loveland.

We have 3 acres of gardens that may be toured during your wine tasting. Presently we have 4 acres of vineyards and plan on additional plantings in the coming years. We encourage our guests to bring wine tasting snacks to enjoy during the tastings. If possible, we ask for 8 or more tasters per appointment.

TASTING ROOM INFORMATION: By appointment only

DIRECTIONS: Directions will be provided at time of tasting appointment confirmation.

OTHER AMENITIES AT WINERY: Beautiful gardens behind our Winery with a deck overlooking the lake with Rocky Mountain National Park and Indian Peaks Wilderness as the backdrop.

WINE AVAILABLE FOR PURCHASE OUTSIDE OF WINERY: Yes

OTHER TASTING ROOM LOCATIONS: Estes Park Farmers Market, Elkhorn Avenue, Estes Park, CO 80517; Larimer County Farmers Market, 200 W. Oak Street, Ft. Collins, CO 80521; Opera Galleria, 123 N College Ave, Fort Collins, CO 80524 (winter)

NOTES: ____

____

____

____

BLUE SKIES WINERY

251 Jefferson Street, Fort Collins, CO 80524
970-407-9463
blueskieswinery.com
info@blueskieswinery.com

OWNER: Kate and Pat Atkin

YEAR BEGAN OPERATION: 2013

AVERAGE CASES PRODUCED ANNUALLY: Information not Available

WINES PRODUCED:
White: Chardonnay, Gewürztraminer, Pinot Grigio, Viognier
Red: Barbera, Malbec, Pinot Noir, Sangiovese, Tempranillo
Other: Cab/Merlot Blend, Peach Chardonnay, Blackberry Merlot, Raspberry Pinot Noir, Green Apple Riesling

MESSAGE FROM OWNER: Pat and Kate started making wine five years ago at a friend's winery in southern Colorado. They enjoyed it so much, they decided to open their own winery in northern Colorado. Pat loves to talk with people in the tasting room about our wine. Kate loves the art and science of winemaking and prefers to stay in production, monitoring her creations.

We get our grapes from northern California, already crushed and ready to make wine. We are a small batch winery, making our wines bucket to carboy. We generally carry 15 wines in our tasting room, but add "specialty" batches throughout the year.

TASTING ROOM INFORMATION: Monday from 1 to 6 p.m., Wednesday, Thursday and Saturday from noon to 8 p.m., Friday from 1 to 9 p.m., Sunday from noon to 6 p.m. Closed Tuesday.

DIRECTIONS: From I-25 and Exit #269B: Head west on Mulberry Road/Hwy 14; turn right (northwest) onto Riverside Drive (becomes Jefferson Street); the winery is on the left, on the SW corner of Linden and Jefferson Street.

OTHER AMENITIES AT WINERY: No

WINE AVAILABLE FOR PURCHASE OUTSIDE OF WINERY: Yes

OTHER TASTING ROOM LOCATIONS: No

NOTES: ______________________________

____

____

____

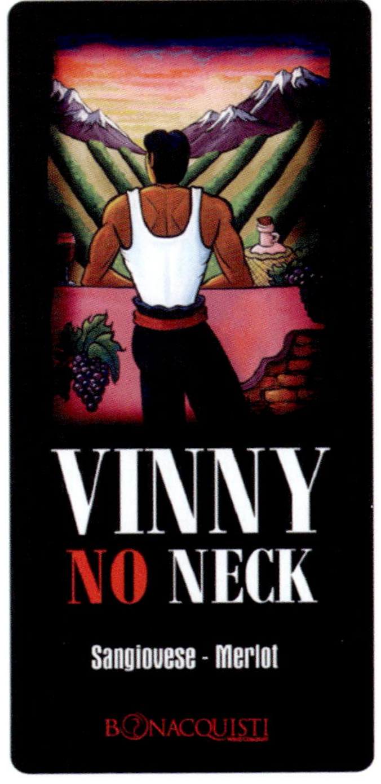

BONACQUISTI WINE COMPANY

4640 Pecos Street, Unit I, Denver CO 80211
303-477-9463
bonacquistiwine.com
paul@denverwine.net

OWNER: Paul and Judi Bonacquisti

YEAR BEGAN OPERATION: 2006

AVERAGE CASES PRODUCED ANNUALLY: 1,500

WINES PRODUCED:
White: Pinot Grigio, Riesling
Red: Cabernet Franc, Cabernet Sauvignon, Sangiovese, Syrah, Zinfandel
Other: Blends called [d] Red, Vinny No Neck and Bella Risa; Port wine

MESSAGE FROM OWNER: Bonacquisti Wine Company opened its doors in October 2006, introducing Denver's Urban Winery to Colorado. Winemaker and Executive Sommelier Paul Bonacquisti is a second generation Italian-American, who learned to make wine from his dad, who learned to make wine from his dad. Bonacquisti creates award-winning wines in various styles: easy drinking, every-night-of-the-week blends and our reserve and limited production varietal wines that are also enjoyable every night of the week.

As a Denver company located in the Sunnyside neighborhood at I-70 and Pecos, Bonacquisti Wine Company supports local education and local art. The winery is a family affair with perennial favorites, Vinny No Neck and Bella Risa, named for our children.

TASTING ROOM INFORMATION: Thursdays from 11 a.m. to 7 p.m., Fridays from 11 a.m. to 9 p.m., Saturdays from 11 a.m. to 5 p.m.

DIRECTIONS: From the intersection of I-70 and Exit #273 (Pecos Street): Head south on Pecos Street; turn left (east) into Colorado Winery Row's parking lot (by Quiznos), which is just north of 46th Avenue.

OTHER AMENITIES AT WINERY: The Winery is available to rent for gatherings up to 100 people.

WINE AVAILABLE FOR PURCHASE OUTSIDE OF WINERY: Yes

OTHER TASTING ROOM LOCATIONS: No

NOTES: ______________________________

____

____

____

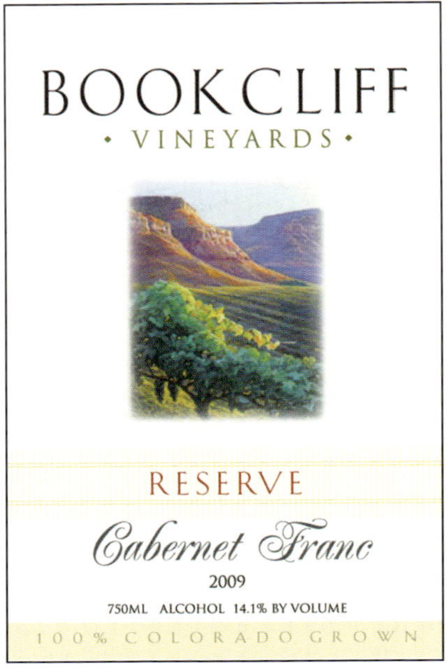

BOOKCLIFF VINEYARDS

1501 Lee Hill Road, Road #17, Boulder, CO 80304
303-449-9463
bookcliffvineyards.com
winery@bookcliffvineyards.com

OWNER: John Garlich and Ulla Merz

YEAR BEGAN OPERATION: 1999

AVERAGE CASES PRODUCED ANNUALLY: 4,200

WINES PRODUCED:
White: Chardonnay, Riesling, Viognier
Red: Cabernet Franc, Cabernet Sauvignon, Malbec, Syrah, Tempranillo
Other: Blends called A Touch of Red, Ensemble, Friday's Folly, Friday's Folly White and several others

MESSAGE FROM OWNER: Bookcliff Vineyards is a Boulder, Colorado, winery making award-winning wines. Our wines are made from 100% Colorado-grown grapes, from our vineyards in Palisade. We own and operate 37 acres of vineyards growing 14 different varieties of grapes, using sustainable farming practices.

John and Ulla, the owners, are both engineers by profession and planted the first six acres of grape vines in 1996, and licensed the winery in 1999. We strive to make wines that are true to the varietal character of the grapes, without adding any color or flavor enhancers. Premier offerings include Ensemble, a Bordeaux-style blend, Cabernet Franc and Malbec. We regularly host local chefs, offering wine- and food-pairing dinners at the winery. BookCliff Vineyards is a member of Boulder Wine Studios with two other wineries in the same complex.

TASTING ROOM INFORMATION: Thursday through Sunday from 1 to 6 p.m.

DIRECTIONS: From Denver: Drive north on 28th Street; turn left (west) onto Lee Hill Road, which is right after the Holiday Drive-In sign. Take the first right into Tamberly Trade Center.

OTHER AMENITIES AT WINERY: Wine-related merchandise for sale and rental space is available for sit-down dinners (up to 36 people) and meeting space (up to 50 people).

WINE AVAILABLE FOR PURCHASE OUTSIDE OF WINERY: Yes

OTHER TASTING ROOM LOCATIONS: The Chocolate Moose and Ice Cream Parlor, 710 Grand Avenue, Glenwwod Springs, CO 81601

NOTES: ____

____

____

____

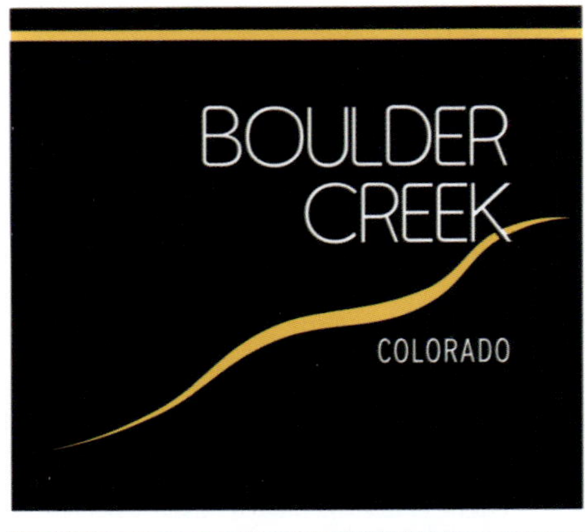

BOULDER CREEK WINERY

6440 Odell Place, Boulder, CO 80301
303-516-9031
bouldercreekwine.com
info@bouldercreekwine.com

OWNER: Jackie and Mike Thompson

YEAR BEGAN OPERATION: 2003

AVERAGE CASES PRODUCED ANNUALLY: 2,000

WINES PRODUCED:
White: Chardonnay, Riesling, Viognier
Red: Cabernet Franc, Cabernet Sauvignon, Merlot, Syrah
Other: Blends called Consensus and Murphy's Choice, Zinfandel Port

MESSAGE FROM OWNER: Founded in 2003 by owner and winemaker Jackie Thompson, Boulder Creek Winery makes "serious" award-winning wines from Colorado grapes. Stop in and see for yourselves. We will exceed your expectations!

TASTING ROOM INFORMATION: Thursday through Sunday from 1 to 5:30 p.m. The winery will be closing on December, 31, 2015 but wine may still be available for purchase via website through 2016.

DIRECTIONS: From the intersection of Hwy 119 (Longmont Diagonal) and 63rd Street in Boulder: Head south on 63rd Street; turn left (east) onto Lookout Road; turn left (north) onto Spine Road; turn left (west) onto Odell Place.

OTHER AMENITIES AT WINERY: Wine-related merchandise

WINE AVAILABLE FOR PURCHASE OUTSIDE OF WINERY: Yes

OTHER TASTING ROOM LOCATIONS: No

NOTES: ____

____

____

____

BOULDER WINE STUDIOS

1501 Lee Hill Drive #14, #16 and #17, Boulder, CO 80304
boulderwinestudios.com
contact@boulderwinestudios.com

Bookcliff Vineyards: 303-449-9463
Settembre Cellars: 303-532-1892
What We Love, The Winery: 303-963-6342

OWNER: Bookcliff Vineyards, Settembre Cellars and What We Love, The Winery

YEAR BEGAN OPERATION: 2014

AVERAGE CASES PRODUCED ANNUALLY: N/A

WINES PRODUCED:
See individual winery websites for more information

MESSAGE FROM OWNER: Experience three Colorado wineries in one afternoon! Boulder Wine Studios is made up of three independent Colorado wineries, each with their own interpretation of Colorado wine. Park once (or bike over from downtown Boulder) and taste at each of the three wineries. Check our website for special events and other group promotions.

TASTING ROOM INFORMATION: Thursday through Sunday from 1 to 6 p.m.

DIRECTIONS: Drive north on 28th Street; turn left (west) onto Lee Hill Road, which is right after the Holiday Drive-In sign. Take the first right into Tamberly Trade Center.

OTHER AMENITIES AT WINERY: Group events for 1 to 100 can be accommodated at Boulder Wine Studios; each winery can accommodate 30 to 40 people; joint events for larger groups is also possible.

WINE AVAILABLE FOR PURCHASE OUTSIDE OF WINERY: Yes

OTHER TASTING ROOM LOCATIONS: No

NOTES: ____

____

____

____

BRANCH OUT CIDER

207 N. Grant Avenue, Fort Collins, CO 80521
970-491-2823
branchoutcider.com
aaron@branchoutcider.com

OWNER: Aaron Fodge and Matt Fater

YEAR BEGAN OPERATION: 2012

AVERAGE CASES PRODUCED ANNUALLY: 250

WINES PRODUCED:
White: None
Red: None
Other: Ciders called: Harvest Hop, Perennial, Tempting Sun

MESSAGE FROM OWNER: Branch Out Cider is the collaboration of neighbors and their beautiful apple trees. Over 200 homeowners in Northern Colorado contribute their apples to these traditional, dry ciders. Our ciders are slowly aged and bottle conditioned with fresh apple juice for a wonderful mouthfeel and dry finish.

TASTING ROOM INFORMATION: By appointment only

DIRECTIONS: Our current location does not have a tasting room, but we are in the process of moving. Please see website for new tasting location.

OTHER AMENITIES AT WINERY: N/A

WINE AVAILABLE FOR PURCHASE OUTSIDE OF WINERY: Yes

OTHER TASTING ROOM LOCATIONS: No

NOTES: ______________________________

____

____

____

CLIMB HARD CIDER

2707 W. Eisenhower Blvd., Loveland, CO 80537
970-744-6891
climbhardcider.com
mail@climbhardcider.com

OWNER: Peter Villeneuve

YEAR BEGAN OPERATION: 2013

AVERAGE CASES PRODUCED ANNUALLY: Information not available

WINES PRODUCED:
White: None
Red: None
Other: Ciders: Apple, Cranberry, Honey, Peach and several seasonals that rotate.

MESSAGE FROM OWNER: We pride ourselves on being an environmentally friendly company. Our ciders, which are primarily light-bodied and sparkling, are distributed in reusable bottles. These products range from dry to sweet, and are made with a variety of apples from the Yakima Valley. The varieties include: Granny Smith, Braeburn, Honeycrisp, Red Delicious, Golden Delicious, Gala and Fuji.

TASTING ROOM INFORMATION: Friday from 2 to 10 p.m., Saturday from noon to 10 p.m., Sunday from 2 to 9 p.m.

DIRECTIONS: From I-25 and Exit #257: Head west on E. Eisenhower Blvd / Hwy 34; the cidery is ¼ mile west of N. Wilson Avenue on your right.

OTHER AMENITIES AT WINERY: Climb Hard Cider merchandise and to-go bottles

WINE AVAILABLE FOR PURCHASE OUTSIDE OF WINERY: No

OTHER TASTING ROOM LOCATIONS: No

NOTES: ____

____

____

____

COLORADO CIDER COMPANY

2650 W. 2nd Avenue #10, Denver, CO 80219
303-759-3560
coloradocider.com
info@coloradocider.com

OWNER: Colorado Cider Company LLC

YEAR BEGAN OPERATION: 2010

AVERAGE CASES PRODUCED ANNUALLY: 10,000

WINES PRODUCED:
White: None
Red: None
Other: Ciders: Glider Cider®, Glider Cider Dry®, Cherry Glider Cider, Grasshop-ah, Newtown Pippin, Ol' Stumpy®, Pome Mel, Pearsnickety®, Uvana®

MESSAGE FROM OWNER: Colorado Cider Company is a craft cidery dedicated to making all juice ciders, with as much Colorado apples as possible. We make dry ciders and showcase the apple flavor over sweetness. The owners are developing an orchard outside Hotchkiss, Colorado and plan on making cider from their traditionally grown cider apple varieties in the future.

TASTING ROOM INFORMATION: Friday from 3 to 6 p.m., Saturday from 2:30 to 6:30 p.m. Other times by appointment only (this is a production facility).

DIRECTIONS: From the intersection of I-25 and Sixth Avenue: Head west on Sixth Avenue; exit at Federal Blvd. heading south; turn left (east) at 2nd Avenue; turn right into the parking lot just before the signal at Bryant Street. We are in the southwest corner of the parking lot.

OTHER AMENITIES AT WINERY: N/A

WINE AVAILABLE FOR PURCHASE OUTSIDE OF WINERY: Yes

OTHER TASTING ROOM LOCATIONS: No

NOTES: ____

____

____

____

COLORADO WINERY ROW

4640 Pecos Street, Denver, CO 80211
coloradowineryrow.com

Bonacquisti Wine Company: 303-477-9463
bonacquistiwine.com
Ryker's Cellars: 720-437-9537
rykerscellars.com

OWNER: Bonacquisti Wine Company and Ryker's Cellars

YEAR BEGAN OPERATION: 2010

AVERAGE CASES PRODUCED ANNUALLY: N/A

WINES PRODUCED:
See individual winery websites for more information.

MESSAGE FROM OWNER: Our two celebrated artisan Colorado wineries are known for producing award-winning wines, including Chardonnay, Riesling, Cabernet Sauvignon, Syrah and other varietal wine. Denver's Urban Wine Tasting Destination™ is conveniently located off of I-70 and Pecos, in the Highlands, just minutes away from LODO and Downtown Denver.

While most of Colorado's grapes are grown on the Western Slope, four hours west of Denver, Colorado Winery Row provides a unique opportunity to taste boutique wines, with proprietors and winemakers. Best of all, you don't have to be a wine geek to gain access to the wine world. Wine tasting without the attitude is our specialty! Come and enjoy local wines in a relaxed, urban setting, with knowledgeable and entertaining hosts, eager to share their passion for wine.

TASTING ROOM INFORMATION: See individual winery websites for specific information

DIRECTIONS: From I-70 and Exit #273 (Pecos Street): Head south on Pecos Street; turn left (east) into Colorado Winery Row parking lot by Quiznos, which is just before 46th Avenue.

OTHER AMENITIES AT WINERY: Local art/mixed media pieces are exhibited throughout; enjoy weekly "Uncorked" events with live music, wines by the glass and select food pairings; Colorado Winery Row is available for private events and wine tasting.

WINE AVAILABLE FOR PURCHASE OUTSIDE OF WINERY: No

OTHER TASTING ROOM LOCATIONS: No

NOTES: ____

____

____

____

COMPASS CIDER HOUSE

216 N. College Avenue, Fort Collins, CO 80524
970-372-1350
compasscider.com
needle@compasscider.com

OWNER: Compass Cider House, Inc.

YEAR BEGAN OPERATION: 2014

AVERAGE CASES PRODUCED ANNUALLY: 4,000

WINES PRODUCED:
White: None
Red: None
Other: Hard Ciders and Perry

MESSAGE FROM OWNER: Compass Cider House produces premium hard ciders and perry in New World Styles. We emphasize quality and innovation and utilize Colorado sourced fruit wherever possible.

TASTING ROOM INFORMATION: Tuesday through Thursday from 4 to 10 p.m., Friday and Saturday from noon to 10 p.m., Sunday noon to 7 p.m.

DIRECTIONS: From I-25 and Exit #269B: Head west on Hwy 14 (Mulberry Street); turn right (north) onto College Avenue; the cidery is on your right in historic downtown Ft. Collins.

OTHER AMENITIES AT WINERY: Full kitchen with daily lunch and pairing menu. Private parties and events also hosted. Live music weekly.

WINE AVAILABLE FOR PURCHASE OUTSIDE OF WINERY: Yes

OTHER TASTING ROOM LOCATIONS: No

NOTES: ____

____

____

____

CREEKSIDE CELLARS

28036 Hwy 74, Evergreen, CO 80439
303-674-5460
creeksidecellars.net
info@creeksidecellars.net

OWNER: Bill and Anita Donahue

YEAR BEGAN OPERATION: 1996

AVERAGE CASES PRODUCED ANNUALLY: 3,000

WINES PRODUCED:
White: Chardonnay, Gewürztraminer, Riesling, Viognier
Red: Cabernet Franc, Cabernet Sauvignon, Merlot, Petit Sirah, Petit Verdot, Syrah,
Other: Blends called Bianco and Rosso; various Port wines

MESSAGE FROM OWNER: Our wines are handcrafted from grapes grown in the Grand Valley AVA of Colorado's Western Slope. All of our wines are produced and bottled at our Evergreen location. At Creekside Cellars, we celebrate the relationship of good food and good wine, shared with family and friends.

Creekside Cellars features a full-service restaurant along with our winery, which overlooks Bear Creek. Stop by for one of our famous antipasto platters and a bottle of wine after snowshoeing, ice skating, hiking or mountain biking!

TASTING ROOM INFORMATION: Daily, from 11 a.m. to 5 p.m.

DIRECTIONS: From the intersection of I-70 and Exit #252 (westbound) #251 (eastbound) at the Evergreen/El Rancho exit: Head south on Evergreen Parkway/Hwy 74 approximately 8 miles into town. The winery is on your right (south) side.

OTHER AMENITIES AT WINERY: A café along the banks of Bear Creek; monthly wine pairing dinners; "New Release" parties; available to rent for various events accommodating up to 50 people; catering service.

WINE AVAILABLE FOR PURCHASE OUTSIDE OF WINERY: Yes

OTHER TASTING ROOM LOCATIONS: No

NOTES: ______________________________

____

____

____

DRAGON MEADERY™

2708 S. Helena Way, Aurora, CO 80013
720-371-1970
dragonmeadery.com
info@dragonmeadery.com

OWNER: Shane and Alexandria Fox

YEAR BEGAN OPERATION: 2012

AVERAGE CASES PRODUCED ANNUALLY: 24 cases

WINES PRODUCED:
White: None
Red: None
Other: Meads called: Lavender Metheglin, Paul's' Plagiarized Potion, Raspberry Melomel, Red Apple Cyser, Strawberry Melomel, Traditional Mead

MESSAGE FROM OWNER: Dragon Meadery™ is a small, craft meadery located in Aurora, Colorado. The meadery is owned and operated by Shane and Alexandria Fox, two former chefs who have spent 20 years each in the restaurant and hospitality industry. Having a deep appreciation for food, and respect for the quality of the ingredients, has extended their passion to mead.

Dragon Meadery™ creates craft meads that span the spectrum style, flavors and sweetness. They believe that fresh seasonal produce, honey locally sourced and patience makes the best meads.

TASTING ROOM INFORMATION: By appointment only

DIRECTIONS: Given at time of appointment

OTHER AMENITIES AT WINERY: N/A

WINE AVAILABLE FOR PURCHASE OUTSIDE OF WINERY: Yes

OTHER TASTING ROOM LOCATIONS: No

NOTES: ______________________________

____

____

____

HONEYJACK MEADERY

9769 W. 119th Drive, Bay 7, Broomfield, CO 80021
Dan: 303-746-0193
honeyjack.com
dan@honeyjack.com

OWNER: Dan Bowron and Jimmy Bowron

YEAR BEGAN OPERATION: 2009

AVERAGE CASES PRODUCED ANNUALLY: Information not Available

WINES PRODUCED:
White: None
Red: None
Other: Mead

MESSAGE FROM OWNER: HoneyJack Meadery was started by Dan Bowron, as he enjoyed home winemaking for years. After a decade of perfecting his recipe, he launched HoneyJack Meadery so the public could enjoy his honey wine.

Our mead is 100% all natural, handmade honey wine. Made with fresh organic fruits, we never add sulfites, acids or chemicals of any kind to aid in the fermentation process. We ferment and age naturally in brand-new, toasted oak barrels to give that perfect Old World mead flavor.

TASTING ROOM INFORMATION: By appointment only

DIRECTIONS: From I-25 and Hwy 36 (the Boulder Turnpike): Head west towards Boulder; exit at #121/Wadsworth Boulevard; head south on Wadsworth Boulevard; turn right (west) onto Metro Airport Avenue; turn right (north) onto 119th Drive. The Meadery is located on the west side of the building.

OTHER AMENITIES AT WINERY: We are very small, but can host parties in the summer for up to 100 people.

WINE AVAILABLE FOR PURCHASE OUTSIDE OF WINERY: Yes

OTHER TASTING ROOM LOCATIONS: No

NOTES: ____

____

____

____

RENAISSANCE: noun - a renewal of life, vigor, interest: rebirth: revival

WELCOME TO THE RENAISSANCE

Honey Wine is said to be the oldest known fermented beverage.
In recent years it has begun to regain it's place in History.
We are a small family owned Colorado Meadery and we use honey from our own bees. The Honey Wines we create are great for any event whether big or small, casual or black tie.

PRODUCED AND BOTTLED BY
TWO BEES LLC
SEVERANCE, COLORADO U.S.A.

www.huntersmoonmeadery.com

HUNTERS MOON MEADERY

Artwork by: kelly apgar

EARL GREG

SEMI-SWEET HONEY WINE WITH SPICE ADDED

ALCOHOL BY VOLUME 12% 375ML

MADE WITH OUR HONEY AND EARL GREY TEA.THIS HONEY WINE IS VERY LIGHT AND REFRESHING.
SERVE SLIGHTLY CHILLED.
ENJOY RESPONSIBLY,
GREG & KIM

NO SULFITES ADDED
MAY CONTAIN NATURALLY OCCURRING SULFITES.

GOVERNMENT WARNING:
(1) ACCORDING TO THE SURGEON GENERAL, WOMEN SHOULD NOT DRINK ALCOHOLIC BEVERAGES DURING PREGNANCY BECAUSE OF THE RISK OF BIRTH DEFECTS.
(2) CONSUMPTION OF ALCOHOLIC BEVERAGES IMPAIRS YOUR ABILITY TO DRIVE A CAR OR OPERATE MACHINERY, AND MAY CAUSE HEALTH PROBLEMS.

HUNTERS MOON MEADERY

404 Immigrant Trail, Severance, CO 80550
970-302-3183
huntersmoonmeadery.com
kim@huntersmoonmeadery.com

OWNER: Greg and Kim Bowdish

YEAR BEGAN OPERATION: 2010

AVERAGE CASES PRODUCED ANNUALLY: 500

WINES PRODUCED:
White: None
Red: None
Other: Blueberry Haze, Earl Greg, Howling Moon, Kim's Clove, Kona Mikala, Lunar Lemon, Moon Dance Cherry, Mountain Berry, Prospector Peach, Sweet Mountain Berry, Touch of Gold, Trappers Cask, Trappers Cask Red

MESSAGE FROM OWNER: We are a family-owned Meadery/Honey Winery on the North Front Range of Colorado. We started production in December, 2010. We do not rush our meads, we prefer to age our meads for 8 – 18 months before bottling. The majority of our meads are semi-sweet, although we have some that are dry, off-dry and sweet as well.

We use honey from our 60 beehives to make our meads. Grapes are not used in the fermentation of meads, but we will be producing two different mead/grape wine blends (call Pyments) in 2015. We currently have 13 meads in our line up and will be adding a few more this year. In four years we have competed in five competitions and have been awarded nine International and four Colorado medals.

TASTING ROOM INFORMATION: By appointment only

DIRECTIONS: Please call for directions, as our facility is in a residential area.

OTHER AMENITIES AT WINERY: N/A

WINE AVAILABLE FOR PURCHASE OUTSIDE OF WINERY: Yes

OTHER TASTING ROOM LOCATIONS: No

NOTES: ____

____

____

____

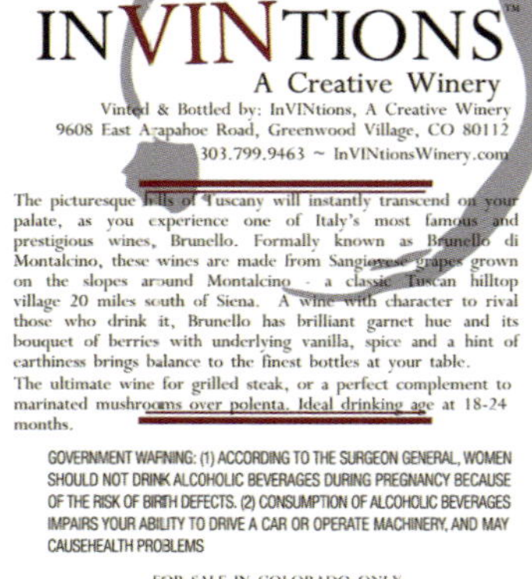

InVINtions WINERY

9608 E. Arapahoe Road, Greenwood Village, CO 80112
303-799-9463
invintionswinery.com
info@invintionswinery.com

OWNER: Marcus Tipton

YEAR BEGAN OPERATION: 2010

AVERAGE CASES PRODUCED ANNUALLY: Information not Available

WINES PRODUCED:
White: Chardonnay, Fume Blanc, Pinot Gris, Riesling, Viognier
Red: Amarone, Barolo, Cabernet Sauvignon, Carmenere, Malbec, Merlot, Pinot Noir, Shiraz, Tempranillo, Zinfandel
Other: Italian Red Blends, Frruit Wines, Hard Apple Ciders

MESSAGE FROM OWNER: Our winery is a locally, family-owned and operated business run by third and fourth generation Coloradoans. Our fully operational winery is located in the heart of the DTC area in Greenwood Village. We are an actual winemaking operation, run by an award-winning, German trained, winemaker. The grapes for our wines arrive from all over the world and are low in sulfites and fruit forward, in the European tradition. The wines are meant to be enjoyed young, and age beautifully within just a few years. We have nearly 100 wines to choose from and everything is open for tasting.

Enjoy our wines by the glass, by the bottle, or we invite you to become the vintner and create your own batch of wine (28 bottles)! Custom labeled wine makes a perfect gift for the holidays, friends and family, as well as business associates or corporate gifting. Custom labeled wine isn't just for that special day; it can make ANY day special! Visit our winery today and uncork the experience of wine tasting and making custom labeled wine.

TASTING ROOM INFORMATION: Tuesday through Saturday from noon to 8 p.m.

DIRECTIONS: From I-25 and Exit #197 (Arapahoe Road): Head east on Arapahoe Road 2 ½ blocks; turn right (south) onto Clinton Court; turn left (east) into the parking area.

OTHER AMENITIES AT WINERY: Wine-related merchandise; private event/meeting space; Technical wine tasting courses; Custom Wine Labels and Winemaking Experiences.

WINE AVAILABLE FOR PURCHASE OUTSIDE OF WINERY: Yes

OTHER TASTING ROOM LOCATIONS: No

NOTES: ____

____

____

____

KINGMAN ESTATES WINERY

800 East 64th Avenue, Denver, CO 80229
Mailing address: 2319 Fairfax Street, Denver, CO 80207
720-560-7270
kingmanwine.com
info@kingmanwine.com

OWNER: Karen and Doug Kingman

YEAR BEGAN OPERATION: 2011

AVERAGE CASES PRODUCED ANNUALLY: 3,000

WINES PRODUCED:
White: Chardonnay, Riesling, Viognier
Red: Cabernet Franc, Cabernet Sauvignon, Merlot, Zinfandel
Other: Blends called: Felicity, Marv'lous-1680, Mysterium, Nefarious Red

MESSAGE FROM OWNER: It all started with ten acres and a barn located between Grand Junction and Palisade. Unfortunately we discovered the ground would not easily grow grapes and that commuting from Denver was not sustainable, so we sold the property. In August of 2011 we opened our Denver tasting room and have been steadily running out of space ever since!

We purchase most of our grapes from great vineyards in the Palisade area, such as Whitewater Hill and Bookcliff Vineyards. All our wines are crafted at our Denver winery from grapes delivered immediately to the winery after picking. The grapes are processed in the parking lot in front of the winery and fermented in tanks inside. We age our Vintage wines in stainless tanks with oak additions for the red wines and our Reserve red wines are aged in oak barrels two to three years before bottling.

Stop by the winery the first weekend of each month for a taste of our special Reserve wines.

TASTING ROOM INFORMATION: Winter, Saturday and Sunday from noon to 5 p.m., Summer, Saturday from 2 to 7 p.m., Sunday from noon to 5 p.m. Closed Easter, Thanksgiving, and Christmas.

DIRECTIONS: From I-25 and Exit #215: Head east on 58th Street; turn left (north) onto Washington Street; turn right (east) onto 64th Avenue; take the second entrance into the parking lot on the right; the winery is in front of you.

OTHER AMENITIES AT WINERY: Facility rental from 40 people (sitting) to 65 (standing), Barrel tasting and Harvest Festival events, Volunteer bottling and crush opportunities, winery tours, local art and merchandise.

WINE AVAILABLE FOR PURCHASE OUTSIDE OF WINERY: Yes

OTHER TASTING ROOM LOCATIONS: No

NOTES: ______________________________

____

____

____

MEDOVINA

Mailing address: P.O. Box 629, Niwot, CO 80544
303-845-3090
medovina.com
mead@medovina.com

OWNER: Mark and Kellie Beran

YEAR BEGAN OPERATION: Information not Available

AVERAGE CASES PRODUCED ANNUALLY: Information not Available

WINES PRODUCED:
White: None
Red: None
Other: Meads - Dry, Off-Dry, Semi-Sweet and Dessert; Hard Cider

MESSAGE FROM OWNER: Medovina brings you artisan Colorado Honey Wine, produced by our meadmaster, Mark Beran, and his dedicated work force of Buckfast bees, now over half a million strong. Medovina produces its own honey, from which it handcrafts its mead. Our beeyards are nestled in Old Town Niwot – in the shade of large cottonwoods planted nearly a century ago by early homesteaders.

As summer gives way to autumn, Medovina begins harvesting the honey and crafting its mead. Our Old World process preserves the rich floral extracts present in our honey. Our meads are produced naturally, without filtering or added sulfites. Alcohol, honey and acidity are harmonized by producing our meads slowly, in small batches, and barrel aging them before bottling. Further aging occurs naturally in the bottle and full maturity can be expected in three to eight years, but you do not have to wait that long to enjoy them. Drink Mead, save a honey bee!

TASTING ROOM INFORMATION: By appointment only

DIRECTIONS: Given at time of appointment

OTHER AMENITIES AT WINERY: Private tasting seminars

WINE AVAILABLE FOR PURCHASE OUTSIDE OF WINERY: Yes

OTHER TASTING ROOM LOCATIONS: No

NOTES: ____

____

____

____

MILE HIGH WINERY

2811 Walnut Street, Denver, CO 80205
Mailing address: PO Box 2395, Fraser, CO 80442
303-296-9463
milehighwinery.com
jon@milehighwinery.com

OWNER: Jon Brickner

YEAR BEGAN OPERATION: 2013

AVERAGE CASES PRODUCED ANNUALLY: 2,000

WINES PRODUCED:
White: Chardonnay, Riesling, Sauvignon Blanc
Red: Cabernet Sauvignon, Merlot, Tempranillo, Zinfandel
Other: Port

MESSAGE FROM OWNER: I am a second generation winemaker and everyone in my family is a winemaker. My wines are handcrafted and made on a small scale. Come by for some premium, handcrafted wine in a very relaxed, comfortable tasting room in the RiNo district.

TASTING ROOM INFORMATION: Tuesday through Friday from 4 to 10 p.m., Saturday from 1 to 10 p.m., Sunday 1 to 5 p.m.; closed Monday

DIRECTIONS: From I-25 and Exit 212C: Head southeast on 20th Street; turn left (northeast) onto Market Street (which becomes Walnut Street at Broadway); the winery will be on your left.

OTHER AMENITIES AT WINERY: Facilities for meetings, banquets and small weddings.

WINE AVAILABLE FOR PURCHASE OUTSIDE OF WINERY: Yes

OTHER TASTING ROOM LOCATIONS: No

NOTES: ____

____

____

____

POINT BLANK WINERY

6547 S. Racine Circle, Suite 1400, Centennial, CO 80111
720-328-2513
pointblankwinery.com
drinkwhatyoulike@pointblankwinery.com

OWNER: Erin Ozgen

YEAR BEGAN OPERATION: 2011

AVERAGE CASES PRODUCED ANNUALLY: Information not Available

WINES PRODUCED:
White: Seasonal rotations
Red: Seasonal rotations
Other: Seasonal rotations

MESSAGE FROM OWNER: Point Blank Winery is a microwinery that was founded in 2011 and opened its Tasting Room in December 2012. The winery's focus is on small-batch craft winemaking. All wines are fermented, finished and bottled at the winery, and the Tasting Room is perfect for small- to medium-sized groups and private events.

TASTING ROOM INFORMATION: Saturday from 1 to 6 p.m.

DIRECTIONS: From I-25 and Arapahoe Road: Head east on Arapahoe Road; turn left (north) onto S. Peoria Street; at traffic circle make an immediate right (east) onto E. Peakview Avenue; turn right (southeast) onto S. Racine Circle; the winery is on your right in Arapahoe Corporate Park II.

OTHER AMENITIES AT WINERY: The Tasting Room is available for private events. The winery does not serve food at this time; however, you are more than welcome to bring your own food or to order-in once you arrive.

WINE AVAILABLE FOR PURCHASE OUTSIDE OF WINERY: No

OTHER TASTING ROOM LOCATIONS: No

NOTES: ____

____

____

____

PURGATORY CELLARS WINERY

18921 Plaza Drive, Suite 100, Parker, CO 80134
303-990-7002
purgatorycellarscolorado.com
info@purgatorycellars.net

OWNER: Marko Ćopić and Gary Tassler

YEAR BEGAN OPERATION: 2014

AVERAGE CASES PRODUCED ANNUALLY: Information not Available

WINES PRODUCED:
White: Chardonnay, Reisling, Roussanne
Red: Malbec, Petit Sirah, Sangiovese, Zinfandel
Other: Amphora

MESSAGE FROM OWNER: Owner Marko Ćopić originates from Jastrebarsko, Croatia and brings 20 years of "Old World" and Mediterranean winemaking experience to Colorado, combining them with his modern winemaking techniques to offer a vastly different wine tasting experience to the Colorado viticultural scene. Purgatory Cellars works hard to source most of their grapes from Colorado and to exploit the qualities of Colorado's unique climate and significant elevation features. The winery is working to bring specific qualities of grapes from the Western Slopes and Four Corners regions of Colorado to the Front Range.

Purgatory Cellars is making and aging wine in Amphora containers, with their origin dating back about 5,000 years in ancient Greek and Roman history. These containers were used in the preservation and transportation of various products, both liquid and dry, but mainly for winemaking. The Amphorae are made from special clay in the country of Georgia and infused with beeswax and then baked in a wood-fired kiln until the beeswax is completely infused in the pot. This winemaking technique provides flavors and characteristics different from other aging methods. Our Amphora production will be about 3,000 liters per year and include at least 5 different varietals.

TASTING ROOM INFORMATION: Monday through Thursday from noon to 9 p.m., Friday and Saturday from 10 a.m. to 11 p.m., Sunday from noon to 9 p.m.

DIRECTIONS: From I-25 and Lincoln Avenue: Head east on Lincoln Avenue; turn right (south) onto Dransfeldt Road; turn left (east) onto Plaza Drive; turn left (north) onto S. Progress Way; the winery is on your immediate left.

OTHER AMENITIES AT WINERY: Available for small meetings and private party reservations.

WINE AVAILABLE FOR PURCHASE OUTSIDE OF WINERY: Yes

OTHER TASTING ROOM LOCATIONS: No

NOTES: ____

____

____

REDSTONE MEADERY

4700 Pearl Street, Boulder, CO 80301
720-406-1215
redstonemeadery.com
info@redstonemeadery.com

OWNER: David Myers

YEAR BEGAN OPERATION: 2000

AVERAGE CASES PRODUCED ANNUALLY: 120,000 liters (we bottle and keg our meads)

WINES PRODUCED:
White: None
Red: None
Other: Mead - Nectars, Mountain Honey wines and Reserve Dessert Meads

MESSAGE FROM OWNER: David Myers, known as "Chairman of the Mead," founder of Redstone Meadery, is a romantic and wants to see mead once again enjoying the glory days of yesteryear. He started the Boulder, Colorado company with the "natural philosophy" that he produce the highest quality honey wine on the market. Because of this "philosophy of mead," Redstone does not cork, but instead uses swing top bottles. In keeping with the "natural" approach, Redstone does not add any sulfites, uses only all natural ingredients and is 100% gluten-free.

Redstone only pasteurizes the must (unfermented mead) and never boils. Redstone specializes in medium to dry style meads and offers complimentary tastings of many of their award-winning meads. Remember to...Ask for Mead!

TASTING ROOM INFORMATION: Monday through Friday from noon to 6:30 p.m., Saturday from noon to 5 p.m.

DIRECTIONS: From the intersection of Hwy 36 (Boulder Turnpike) and Foothills Parkway: Head north on Foothills Parkway; take the Pearl Street exit; turn right onto Pearl Parkway at the bottom of the ramp; take an immediate left onto 47th Street; turn right (east) onto Pearl Street. The Meadery is on the right (south) side of the street.

OTHER AMENITIES AT WINERY: Winery tours (1 & 3 p.m. weekdays, 12:30 p.m. Saturdays); Mead-related merchandise; Saturday afternoon live music from 1:30 to 4:30 p.m. from November through April (free).

WINE AVAILABLE FOR PURCHASE OUTSIDE OF WINERY: Yes

OTHER TASTING ROOM LOCATIONS: No

NOTES: ____

____

____

____

RIVER GARDEN WINERY

9490 County Road 25, Fort Lupton, CO 80621
303-304-4064
rivergardenwinery.com
rgwinery@gmail.com

OWNER: Robert and Mary Stahl

YEAR BEGAN OPERATION: 2008

AVERAGE CASES PRODUCED ANNUALLY: 500

WINES PRODUCED:
White: LaCrosse, LaCrescent
Red: Cabernet Sauvignon, Chancellor, Frontenac, Malbec, Marechal Foch, Marquette, Merlot, Petit Sirah, Primitivo, Sangiovese, Syrah, Tempranillo
Other: Blend called: Water Dance White; Cherry, Rhubarb, Cranberry, Pumpkin Spice wines

MESSAGE FROM OWNER: Bob and Mary Stahl moved to Colorado in 1978 from NW Ohio where they grew up on farms. Mary works in downtown Denver in the oil and gas industry and has over 30 years' experience as a Geo-tech. Bob left working for the State of Colorado after 22 years of public service in 2011 to begin construction of the winery building.

In the spring of 2005 the first acre of eight different grape varietals were planted, and that has gradually expanded to five acres. Bob began making wine commercially in 2008 as the first grapes became available. All of our wines are produced at the winery and are only available here. We have wines made from our own grapes as well as grapes brought over from the Western Slope and Washington State. We are not the usual winery located in a warehouse in an industrial area, we are in the country along the Platte River with old cottonwoods and an abundance of wildlife. Deer, bald eagles, wild turkeys, great horned owls and great blue herons are regular visitors here.

TASTING ROOM INFORMATION: Saturday from noon to 5 p.m., closed January; other times by appointment

DIRECTIONS: From I-25 and Exit #235: Head east on Mineral Road/ Hwy 52; turn left (north) onto Hwy 85; turn left (west) onto CR 18; turn right (north) onto CR 25; in 1.5 miles look for the winery sign on the right.

OTHER AMENITIES AT WINERY: Tasting room will hold up to 100 guests for meetings, weddings, receptions and parties. Outside area is available for more than 100, and our spacious deck is a great place to have a picnic.

WINE AVAILABLE FOR PURCHASE OUTSIDE OF WINERY: No

OTHER TASTING ROOM LOCATIONS: No

NOTES: ____________________

____

____

____

RUBY TRUST CELLARS

864 W. Happy Canyon Road #120, Castle Rock, CO 80108
720-202-2041
rubytrustcellars.com
info@rubytrustcellars.com

OWNER: Ray and Jean Bruening

YEAR BEGAN OPERATION: 2009

AVERAGE CASES PRODUCED ANNUALLY: 400 - 500

WINES PRODUCED:
White: None
Red: None
Other: Red blends focusing on Syrah, Cabernet Franc and Petit Verdot

MESSAGE FROM OWNER: Founded in 2009, Ruby Trust Cellars is a boutique winery located in picturesque Castle Rock, Colorado. We are focusing on small production, hand-crafted Colorado red wine blends.

TASTING ROOM INFORMATION: By appointment only

DIRECTIONS: From I-25 at Exit #187: Head southwest on Happy Canyon Road; just before Hwy 85, turn left (south) into the Village at Castle Pines shops. We are located behind the shops at #120.

OTHER AMENITIES AT WINERY: N/A

WINE AVAILABLE FOR PURCHASE OUTSIDE OF WINERY: Yes

OTHER TASTING ROOM LOCATIONS: No

NOTES: ____

____

____

____

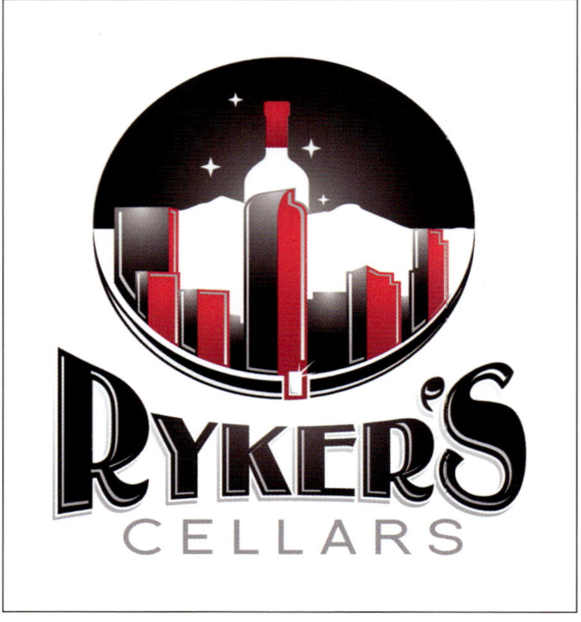

RYKER'S CELLARS

4640 Pecos Street, Unit G, Denver, CO 80211
720-437-9537
rykerscellars.com
rykerscellars@gmail.com

OWNER: Ryker Brandt

YEAR BEGAN OPERATION: 2013

AVERAGE CASES PRODUCED ANNUALLY: Information not available

WINES PRODUCED:
White: Chardonnay, Riesling, Sauvignon Blanc
Red: Cabernet Sauvignon, Malbec, Petite Sirah
Other: Blends called: Doggles White, Doggles Red; Rosé

MESSAGE FROM OWNER: Ryker Brandt loved wine from his first taste of a brilliant Chateaneuf-du-Pape while working at an award winning bistro with a 5,000 bottle wine cellar. That taste caused him to pack his bags and head West, first on a road trip, then as a destination where he found a landing place in Santa Cruz, California, otherwise known as the central coast of California wine country. Ryker showed up at the winery during harvest and begged for a job crushing grapes and doing punchdowns. That was the start of his cellar work and professional winemaking career!

TASTING ROOM INFORMATION: Thursday through Saturday from noon to 7 p.m.; other times by appointment

DIRECTIONS: From I-70 and Exit #273 (Pecos Street): Head south on Pecos Street; turn left (east) into Colorado Winery Row's parking lot by Quiznos, which is just before 46th Avenue.

OTHER AMENITIES AT WINERY: Room is available for meetings or classes

WINE AVAILABLE FOR PURCHASE OUTSIDE OF WINERY: Yes

OTHER TASTING ROOM LOCATIONS: No

NOTES: ____

____

____

____

ST. VRAIN VINEYARDS AND WINERY

1633 S. Hwy 287, Berthoud, CO 80513
303-929-2958
Website: N/A
jayemmons@msn.com

OWNER: Roy Emmons

YEAR BEGAN OPERATION: 2003

AVERAGE CASES PRODUCED ANNUALLY: 200

WINES PRODUCED:
White: Chardonnay
Red: Merlot
Other: Blends called Little River Red, St. Vrain Reserve Red, Roy's Red, Cathy's White, Twinkle Twinkle and Plum wine

MESSAGE FROM OWNER: Owner, Roy Emmons, is a former brewmaster, who started the winery in 1998. He grows his own cold-hardy, French hybrid grapes for his wine production, obtaining additional grapes from a number of sources. Taste our delicious wines at the Longmont Farmers Market.

TASTING ROOM INFORMATION: N/A

DIRECTIONS: N/A

OTHER AMENITIES AT WINERY: N/A

WINE AVAILABLE FOR PURCHASE OUTSIDE OF WINERY: No

OTHER TASTING ROOM LOCATIONS: Longmont Farmers Market, 9595 Nelson Road, Longmont, CO 80501

NOTES: ____

____

____

____

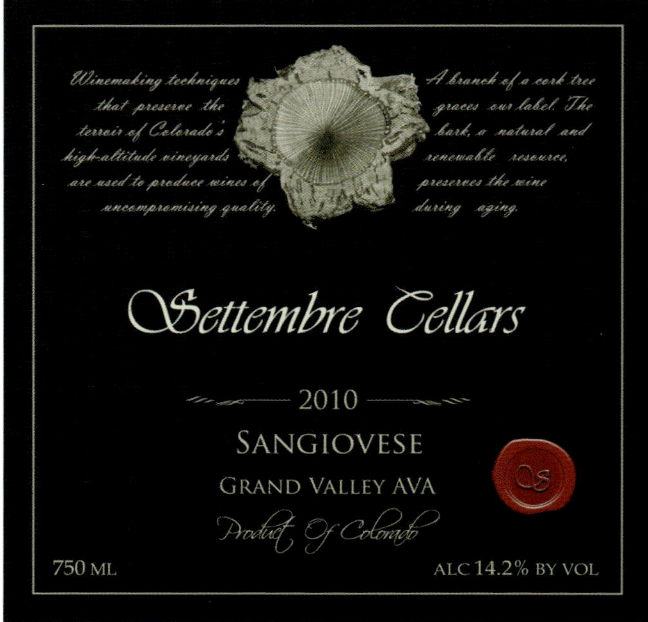

SETTEMBRE CELLARS

1501 Lee Hill Drive #16, Boulder, CO 80304
303-532-1892
settembrecellars.com
contact@settembrecellars.com

OWNER: Blake and Tracy Eliasson

YEAR BEGAN OPERATION: 2007

AVERAGE CASES PRODUCED ANNUALLY: 500

WINES PRODUCED:
White: Chardonnay, Riesling
Red: Cabernet Sauvignon, Sangiovese, Syrah
Other: Rosato

MESSAGE FROM OWNER: Blake and Tracy Eliasson have been handcrafting elegant, food-friendly wines from Colorado grapes since 2007. With an uncompromising commitment to quality, and winemaking techniques influenced by winemakers in Italy and France, their wines showcase the unique terroir of Colorado's high-altitude vineyards. We balance art, science and patience to produce nuanced wines of elegance, balance and depth.

Owners Blake and Tracy fell in love eating and drinking Italian food and wine. We made homemade pasta and basil pesto on our second date, were married in September and honeymooned in Italy. Settembre is Italian for September, a name that honors these influences.

TASTING ROOM INFORMATION: Thursday through Sunday from 1 to 6 p.m.

DIRECTIONS: From Denver: Drive north on 28th Street; turn left (west) onto Lee Hill Road, which is right after the Holiday Drive-In sign. Take the first right into Tamberly Trade Center.

OTHER AMENITIES AT WINERY: Private events for 2 – 30 people where you can work with our caterers, choose your own or self-cater. Bring a snack or meal to enjoy with our wines and have yourself an indoor urban picnic.

WINE AVAILABLE FOR PURCHASE OUTSIDE OF WINERY: Yes

OTHER TASTING ROOM LOCATIONS: 63rd Street Farm, 3795 63rd Street, Boulder, CO 80301, on various dates. See our website.

NOTES: ____

____

____

____

SILVER VINES WINERY

7509 Grandview Avenue, Arvada, CO 80002
303-456-5212
silvervineswinery.com
winery@silvervineswinery.com

OWNER: Danny and Jeff Chayer

YEAR BEGAN OPERATION: 2011

AVERAGE CASES PRODUCED ANNUALLY: Information not available

WINES PRODUCED:
White: Chardonnay, Pinot Grigio, Riesling
Red: Cabernet Franc, Cabernet Sauvignon, Merlot, Primitivo, Syrah
Other: Blends called: Rocky White, Rocky Red, Rocky Delight; dessert wine

MESSAGE FROM OWNER: Danny and Jeff are from Minnesota and moved to Colorado in 2011 to open Silver Vines Winery. Both have worked at several wineries in Minnesota, Washington and Texas. We buy grapes from Colorado, California and Washington and make our wine at our warehouse in Arvada.

We have won several awards in International competitions in California, New York and Florida. Our Colorado grown Primitivo took a double gold in the 2014 Finger Lakes competition in New York. Our Chocolate delight dessert wine also took a double gold in the same competition the year before.

Our winery is located in Olde Town Arvada, which hosts street festivals all year. We also have a wine club that anyone can enjoy!

TASTING ROOM INFORMATION: Monday through Thursday from 11 a.m. to 10 p.m., Friday and Saturday from 11 a.m. to 1 a.m., Sunday from noon to 9 p.m.

DIRECTIONS: From I-70 and Wadsworth Blvd: Take Wadsworth Blvd / Hwy 121 north; turn left (northwest) onto W. 53rd Avenue (which turns into Olde Wadsworth Blvd); turn right (east) onto Grandview Avenue; the winery is on your left.

OTHER AMENITIES AT WINERY: Wine-related merchandise; small room available to host meetings and parties.

WINE AVAILABLE FOR PURCHASE OUTSIDE OF WINERY: Yes

OTHER TASTING ROOM LOCATIONS: No

NOTES: ____

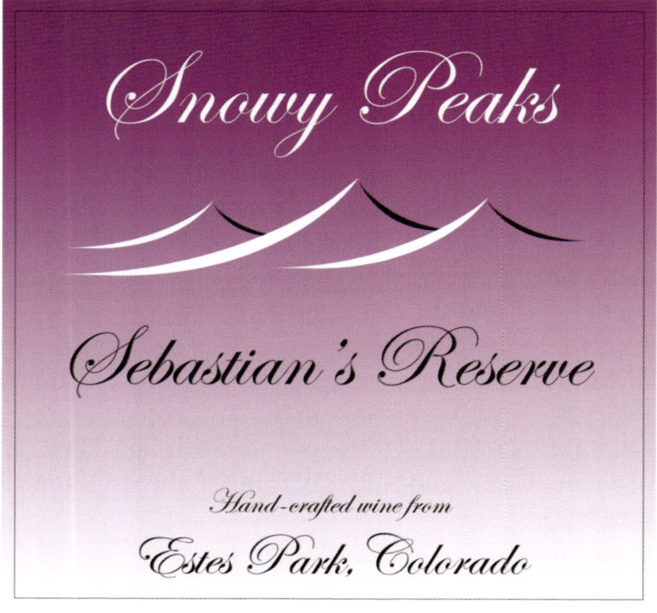

SNOWY PEAKS WINERY

292 Moraine Avenue, Estes Park, CO 80517
970-586-2099
snowypeakswinery.com
info@snowypeakswinery.com

OWNER: Erik and Candice Mohr

YEAR BEGAN OPERATION: 2005

AVERAGE CASES PRODUCED ANNUALLY: 1,200

WINES PRODUCED:
White: Riesling, Rousanne, Viognier
Red: Cabernet Franc, Cabernet Sauvignon, Merlot, Mourvèdre, Petite Sirah, Syrah
Other: Several white and red blends; Rosé; Dessert wines

MESSAGE FROM OWNER: Taking inspiration from a business partner, Erik and a skeptical Candice decided to start Snowy Peaks Winery in 2004. After months of searching high and low for a building, our future was sealed in Estes Park! We opened our doors in 2005 with no wine of our own but a selection from other Colorado wineries. We bought grapes from growers on the Western Slope that fall and released our first wine in 2006. Since then we have steadily increased the quantity and variety of our offerings.

During the summer season, we generally have 18 Snowy Peaks wines to taste, plus an array of other Colorado wines. Our focus has always been on small batches of well-crafted wines, with a diversity of styles that appeal to all palates. Our tasting room staff tries to keep tastings fun and casual, with the knowledge to educate, if asked.

We believe it's not about us, but you and what you like! Bring the kids along, they will have a great time in the "No Wine-ing Zone," our designated playroom.

TASTING ROOM INFORMATION: Memorial Day to Labor Day, Monday through Saturday from 11 a.m. to 7:00 p.m., Sunday from 12:30 to 6 p.m.; September to May open daily, call ahead for hours.

DIRECTIONS: From the intersection of Hwy 34 and Hwy 36 in Estes Park: Head west into downtown Estes Park; turn left (south) onto Moraine Avenue (Hwy 36).

OTHER AMENITIES AT WINERY: Colorado-made food products, handcrafted gifts from local artisans and wine-related merchandise.

WINE AVAILABLE FOR PURCHASE OUTSIDE OF WINERY: Yes

OTHER TASTING ROOM LOCATIONS: No

NOTES: ____

____

____

____

SPERO WINERY

3316 W. 64th Avenue, Denver, CO 80221
720-519-1506
sperowinery.biz
sperowinery@aol.com

OWNER: Clyde and June Spero

YEAR BEGAN OPERATION: 1999

AVERAGE CASES PRODUCED ANNUALLY: 2,100

WINES PRODUCED:
White: Cayuga White, Chardonnay, Colombard, Malvasia Bianca, Muscat, Riesling, Viognier
Red: Barbera, Cabernet Franc, Cabernet Sauvignon, Chancellor, Malbec, Merlot, Sangiovese, Syrah, Zinfandel
Other: Pomegranate and Dessert wines

MESSAGE FROM OWNER: Spero Winery is a family-owned and operated boutique winery, with wines made in the "Old World" tradition. Clyde Spero, winemaker, has been making wine all of his life; a craft he learned from his father, who emigrated from Potenza, Italy. Our friendly and relaxed tasting room is open Saturdays for free wine tasting. Here you can enjoy the rich and full-bodied wines made more in a European tradition, with our red wines being aged a minimum of two years in oak. We are sure you will find a favorite in the 20+ varieties we offer!

There are special case discounts, and don't forget to return the Spero wine bottles for your $1 per bottle credit towards your next purchase. Come enjoy the relaxed, "old country" feel of our tasting room, a great place to bring family and friends!

TASTING ROOM INFORMATION: Saturday from 1 to 5 p.m. or by appointment.

DIRECTIONS: From the intersection of Federal Boulevard and W. 64th Avenue in Denver: Head west on W. 64th Avenue 3 blocks. Winery is on the left (south) side of the street.

OTHER AMENITIES AT WINERY: Private tasting parties for 20–50 people

WINE AVAILABLE FOR PURCHASE OUTSIDE OF WINERY: Yes

OTHER TASTING ROOM LOCATIONS: No

NOTES: ______________________________

____

____

____

STEM CIDERS

2811 Walnut Street, Suite 150, Denver, CO 80205
720-443-3007
stemciders.com
info@stemciders.com

OWNER: Eric Foster and Phil Kao

YEAR BEGAN OPERATION: 2014

AVERAGE CASES PRODUCED ANNUALLY: Information not available

WINES PRODUCED:
White: None
Red: None
Other: Ciders called: Banjo, Crabby Neighbor, L'Acier, LcChêne, Malice, Remedy; plus a rotating seasonal

MESSAGE FROM OWNER: Both Eric and Phil come from Michigan, in the heart of apple country, which stemmed their love and appreciation for artisan ciders and quality apples. We hold our growers in the highest regard, and by fostering relationships with them we reward their hard work and promote the re-growth of heirloom apple cultivation.

Located in the heart of the RiNo district, Stem Ciders specializes in dry, hard ciders. We strive to honor the apple's purity and clarity by using traditional cidermaking techniques; the fruit has lots to say if you listen to it carefully! Our barrel program uses traditional methods to complement the flavors and aromas of the fruit with interesting oak characteristics. Come join us to taste what the humble apple has to offer!

TASTING ROOM INFORMATION: Tuesday through Thursday from 4 to 10 p.m., Friday from 3 to 11 p.m., Saturday from noon to 11 p.m., Sunday noon to 8 p.m.

DIRECTIONS: From I-25 and Exit 212C: Head southeast on 20th Street; turn left (northeast) onto Market Street (which becomes Walnut Street at Broadway); turn into Stem Ciders' parking lot, which will be on your left.

OTHER AMENITIES AT WINERY: Each day we offer a different event – from pairings to trivia to music; enjoy food offer by local food trucks; facilities available for private parties.

WINE AVAILABLE FOR PURCHASE OUTSIDE OF WINERY: Yes

OTHER TASTING ROOM LOCATIONS: No

NOTES: ______________________________

____

____

____

SWEETHEART CITY WINES

5500 West Highway 34, Loveland, CO 80537 (Beginning 1/1/16)
970-744-4907
sweetheartcitywines.com
info@sweetheartcitywines.com

OWNER: Jack and Lindsay Cantley and David and Kathy Burks

YEAR BEGAN OPERATION: 2010

AVERAGE CASES PRODUCED ANNUALLY: 1,000 +

WINES PRODUCED:
White: Chardonnay, Riesling, Sauvignon Blanc, Viognier
Red: Cabernet Franc, Cabernet Sauvignon, Malbec, Merlot, Syrah, Tempranillo, Zinfandel
Other: Rosé; Port-style dessert wine

MESSAGE FROM OWNER: Set at the base of the Rocky Mountains next to the Big Thompson River in Loveland, Colorado, Sweetheart City Wines is committed to delivering hand-crafted, small lot wines with a romantic flare celebrating our hometown. We focus on wine production from premium grapes sourced from the finest growing regions in the western United States.

Customers experience our quality wines within our completely unique, elegant timber-framed winery and tasting room, resulting in a rare experience sure to be remembered. We leverage a rich, Old World winemaking family tradition blended with New World techniques to produce top-notch wines with our own Sweetheart City signature.

TASTING ROOM INFORMATION: Grand Opening December, 2015 / Private Tastings & Parties by appointment only until May, 2016. May 1 through October 30, Monday through Saturday from 10 a.m. to 6 p.m., For other times see website.

DIRECTIONS: From I-25 and Exit #257: Take Hwy 34 (E. Eisenhower Blvd) west for 12.5 miles; the winery is just past Wild Lane.

OTHER AMENITIES AT WINERY: Our unique rustic yet elegant venue is perfect for weddings, showers, banquets and corporate meetings and events

WINE AVAILABLE FOR PURCHASE OUTSIDE OF WINERY: Yes

OTHER TASTING ROOM LOCATIONS: No

NOTES: ______________________________

____

____

____

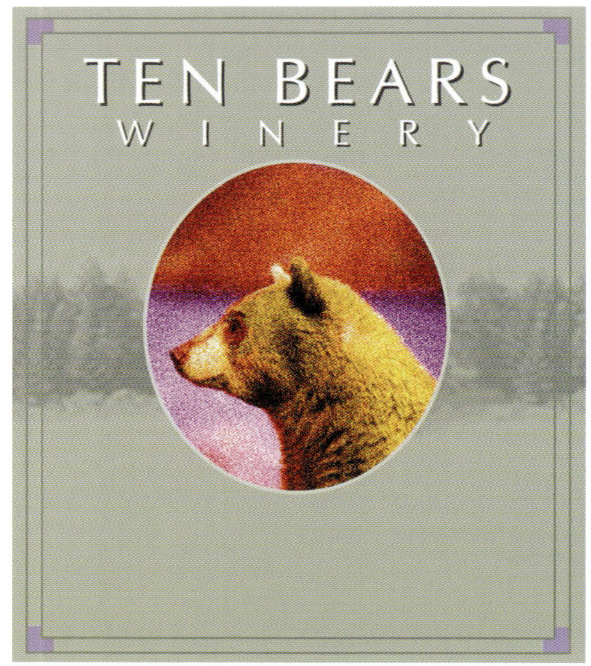

TEN BEARS WINERY

5215 Ten Bears Court, LaPorte, CO 80535
970-566-4043
tenbearswinery.com
tenbearswinery@hotmail.com

OWNER: Bill Conkling

YEAR BEGAN OPERATION: 2006

AVERAGE CASES PRODUCED ANNUALLY: 1,000

WINES PRODUCED:
White: Riesling, American Symphony
Red: Cabernet Sauvignon, Merlot, Pinot Noir
Other: Blends called Cameron Pass White and Poudre River Red Table Wine; Roaming Bear Huckleberry, Pomegranate and Raspberry; Altitude (sparkling); Nutty LaPorte (port); Hard Cider

MESSAGE FROM OWNER: Beware of The Ten Bears! Introduce your palate to a truly superior Colorado wine experience. Our winemaker hand selects only the finest grapes. Using French oak aging and our exclusive "Winter Hibernation Process," we produce smooth and flavorful handcrafted vintages that are easy drinking and never overly tannic. Enjoy!

TASTING ROOM INFORMATION: Wednesday through Saturday from 11 a.m. to 7 p.m.; other days by appointment.

DIRECTIONS: From I-25 at Exit #269 A or B (Hwy 14/Mulberry Street): Head west on Hwy 14/Mulberry Street; turn right (north) onto College Avenue (Hwy 287); turn right (north) and onto Hwy 287 By-Pass (Laramie/Poudre Canyon exit); approximately 4 miles, turn right (northwest) onto CR 56; make an immediate right (northeast) onto 23E; head 1/2 mile to the intersection of 56E and 23E. The winery is a gray building on the right.

OTHER AMENITIES AT WINERY: Home winemaking equipment and other wine items; t-shirts and hats; picnic and patio area; vineyard for touring

WINE AVAILABLE FOR PURCHASE OUTSIDE OF WINERY: Yes

OTHER TASTING ROOM LOCATIONS: Rocky Mountain Oil Olive, 114 N. College Avenue, Ft. Collins, CO 80524

NOTES: ____

____

____

____

THE INFINITE MONKEY THEOREM

3200 Larimer Street, Denver, CO 80205
303-736-8376
theinfinitemonkeytheorem.com
drink@theinfinitemonkeytheorem.com

OWNER: Ben Parsons

YEAR BEGAN OPERATION: 2008

AVERAGE CASES PRODUCED ANNUALLY: 25,000

WINES PRODUCED:
White: Black Muscat, Chardonnay, Gewürztraminer, Riesling, Rousanne, Sauvignon Blanc, Viognier
Red: Cabernet Franc, Cabernet Sauvignon, Malbec, Merlot, Petite Sirah, Petit Verdot, Syrah
Other: Rosé and Blends called The Blindwatchmaker and The 100th Monkey

MESSAGE FROM OWNER: Opened in 2008 in Denver, Colorado, The Infinite Monkey Theorem is an urban winery operating out the RiNo Art District of Denver. The winery's purpose is to use the best grapes, from the highest quality vineyards, to process excellent wines in the heart of the city.

TASTING ROOM INFORMATION: Monday through Friday from 4 to 10 p.m., Saturday from 2 to 9 p.m., Sunday 2 to 8 p.m.

DIRECTIONS: From I-70 exit at Washington Street, which turns into 38th Avenue; turn right (southwest) onto Walnut Street; turn slight right (south) onto Downing Street; turn right (southwest) onto Larimer Street; the winery is on the left..

OTHER AMENITIES AT WINERY: Private parties and tastings; First Friday celebrations

WINE AVAILABLE FOR PURCHASE OUTSIDE OF WINERY: Yes

OTHER TASTING ROOM LOCATIONS: Austin, Texas opening summer of 2015

NOTES: ______________________________

____

____

____

TURQUOISE MESA WINERY

11705 Teller Street, Unit C, Broomfield, CO 80020
303-653-3822
turquoisemesawinery.com
tabwine@aol.com

OWNER: Tom & Mary Joan Bueb

YEAR BEGAN OPERATION: 2004

AVERAGE CASES PRODUCED ANNUALLY: 1,000

WINES PRODUCED:
White: Cayuga, Chardonnay, Fume Blanc, Riesling, Semillon
Red: Cabernet Sauvignon, Merlot, Mourvèdre, Petit Sirah, Sangiovese, Syrah
Other: Blends called Sunset White, Colorado Crimson, TMW Reserve, Vino Turchese, Dessert wines

MESSAGE FROM OWNER: We are a small winery producing award winning, handcrafted wines by a Colorado native. Our wines are made using primarily Colorado grapes. We offer a variety of both red and white wines, including many excellent blends. In our tasting room we offer wine by the glass or bottle. Our wine club offers additional wine discounts to members. Relax in the art nook which features works from Colorado artists. We look forward to meeting you!

TASTING ROOM INFORMATION: Thursday and Saturday from 1 to 6 p.m.; Check website for seasonal times/changes. Other times by appointment.

DIRECTIONS: From Denver: Take US-36/Denver-Boulder Turnpike; exit at 104th Avenue/Church Ranch Blvd.; turn (right) east on 104th/Church Ranch Blvd.; turn left (north) on Westminster Blvd.; turn left (west) onto 116th Avenue; turn right (north) onto Teller Street. Winery is on the left (west) side of the street.

OTHER AMENITIES AT WINERY: N/A

WINE AVAILABLE FOR PURCHASE OUTSIDE OF WINERY: Yes

OTHER TASTING ROOM LOCATIONS: No

NOTES: ______________________________

____

____

____

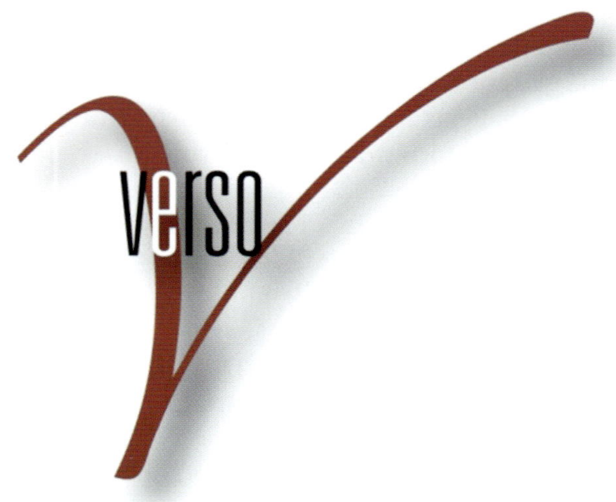

VERSO CELLARS

303-587-9740
versocellars.com
wine@versocellars.com

OWNER: Paul Phillips

YEAR BEGAN OPERATION: 2001

AVERAGE CASES PRODUCED ANNUALLY: 2,000

WINES PRODUCED:
White: None
Red: Cabernet Sauvignon
Other: None

MESSAGE FROM OWNER: Verso Cellars is Colorado's finest 100% Cabernet Sauvignon winery. We grow six varieties of Cabernet grapes, and expertly blend them to craft an extraordinary wine. Our vineyard in East Orchard Mesa makes the most of abundant sunshine, careful attention and precious water to bring you something you may have missed, an excellent Cabernet Sauvignon.

Book a private tasting with owner Paul Phillips by contacting him at 303-587-9740. To purchase Verso Cellars' wine by the glass or bottle, visit Metropolis Coffee.

TASTING ROOM INFORMATION: By appointment only

DIRECTIONS: To Metropolis Coffee at 300 W. 11th Street, Denver, CO 80204. From the intersection of Speer Blvd. and Colfax: Head south on Speer Blvd; turn left (east) onto 11th Avenue; the coffee shop is 2 blocks down on the right..

OTHER AMENITIES AT WINERY: Metropolis Coffee is available to rent for event needs.

WINE AVAILABLE FOR PURCHASE OUTSIDE OF WINERY: Yes

OTHER TASTING ROOM LOCATIONS: Metropolis Coffee, 300 W. 11th Street, Denver, CO 80204

NOTES: ______________________________

____

____

____

WATERS EDGE WINERY – DENVER

2101 E. Arapahoe Road, Suite 101, Centennial, CO 80122
720-381-6663
wewdenver.com
info@wewdenver.com

OWNER: Jennifer and Chad Hulan

YEAR BEGAN OPERATION: 2014

AVERAGE CASES PRODUCED ANNUALLY: Information not available

WINES PRODUCED:
White: Chardonnay, Pinot Grigio, Pinot Gris, Riesling, Sauvignon Blanc, Symphony, Viognier
Red: Cabernet Sauvignon, Merlot, Nebbiolo, Petit Verdot, Pinot Noir, Tempranillo
Other: Several blends, Fruit wines, Ice wines, Ports

MESSAGE FROM OWNER: An urban winery with a minimum footprint, we are able to source our grape must from vineyards all over the world and bring that to our winery in Centennial so we can make some amazing wines! It is our passion for wine, our community and for fun that has allowed us to create Waters Edge Winery – Denver. We partner with a handful of other wineries nationwide to share skills, our love for viticulture and best practices so we are able to make the best wines available in Colorado! We are a winery, a tasting room, a local gathering place for our neighbors (and their dogs!) and great listeners, so stop in for a glass and something to nosh!

TASTING ROOM INFORMATION: Tuesday through Thursday from 11 a.m. to 7 p.m., Friday and Saturday from 11 a.m. to 10 p.m., Sunday from 11 a.m. to 7 p.m., closed Monday.

DIRECTIONS: From the intersection of University Blvd and Arapahoe Road: Head west on Arapahoe Road 2 blocks; the winery is on the right side of the street adjacent to the U.S. Post Office.

OTHER AMENITIES AT WINERY: Available for private events on Mondays for up to 75 people; wine-related food items available for sale.

WINE AVAILABLE FOR PURCHASE OUTSIDE OF WINERY: No

OTHER TASTING ROOM LOCATIONS: No

NOTES: ______________________________

____

____

____

WATER2WINE

8130 S. University Boulevard #110, Centennial, CO 80122
720-489-9463
water2wine.com/denver
denver@water2wine.com

OWNER: The Sample Family

YEAR BEGAN OPERATION: 2006

AVERAGE CASES PRODUCED ANNUALLY: 2,500

WINES PRODUCED:
White: Numerous
Red: Numerous
Other: Nearly 100 varietals, wines and blends to choose from daily

MESSAGE FROM OWNER: Water2Wine is a custom winery that provides a fantastic wine experience. Customers are considered family, and can come to enjoy a glass, a bottle or to make their own custom batch of wine. We like to offer our customers a relaxed atmosphere with knowledgeable and friendly staff and fabulous wines. We are kid and pet friendly and enjoy meeting the entire family!

The original Water2Wine Custom Winery was opened in San Antonio, Texas, in 2003. In 2005, the corporate headquarters was officially established in North Austin. Over the years, Water2Wine has continued to expand its franchising operations across the country with current locations in Texas, Colorado and Wisconsin.

Water2Wine - Centennial was established in 2007 by Derek Handley a local visionary. By July 2012, Derek was ready for a change. The Sample family were long time Wine Club Members and a couple were employees for the former owner. The Samples could not imagine their favorite winery closing and a deal was struck to purchase the winery. The atmosphere is very relaxed and, we hope, welcoming. Our goal is to make everyone feel like family.

TASTING ROOM INFORMATION: Tuesday through Thursday from 2 to 7 p.m., Friday and Saturday from noon to 8 p.m.

DIRECTIONS: From C-470 and University Boulevard: Head north on University Boulevard 2 blocks; winery is on the right (east) side of the street.

OTHER AMENITIES AT WINERY: Available to rent for various events, parties and fund-raisers.

WINE AVAILABLE FOR PURCHASE OUTSIDE OF WINERY: No

OTHER TASTING ROOM LOCATIONS: No

NOTES: ______________________________

____

____

____

WHAT WE LOVE, THE WINERY

1501 Lee Hill Drive, Unit 14, Boulder, CO 80304
303-963-6342
whatwelove.com
info@whatwelove.com

OWNER: Michael Hasler

YEAR BEGAN OPERATION: 2013

AVERAGE CASES PRODUCED ANNUALLY: 3,000

WINES PRODUCED:
White: Chardonnay, Orange Muscat, Sauvignon Blanc
Red: Cabernet Sauvignon, Merlot, Petite Syrah, Syrah, Zinfandel
Other: Red Rhone blend; Sangria; Mulled wine

MESSAGE FROM OWNER: What We Love, The Winery is a craft winery that offers an atmosphere of creativity, fun and adventure with taste! We invite our community to explore new flavors with our innovative products as well as classic varietal wines. We love to offer our winery as a venue for your fundraising efforts, personal celebrations, weddings, intimate dinners or a tasting getaway.

Our star innovatives, the original "Decadent Saint," a hedonistically spiced chocolate and coffee wine liqueur and Decadent Saint Red or White Sangria are a FIRST for the U.S. marketplace…20.5% v/v elixirs designed to be diluted with water, seltzer or champagne to taste. Once opened will stay delicious for months without refrigeration.

Our Wine Alchemist, Michael Hasler, is a studied Enologist with 30 years of experience in Australia, New Zealand, France and the U.S. Explore something completely different in a tasting room!

TASTING ROOM INFORMATION: Thursday through Sunday from 1 to 6 p.m.; other times by appointment

DIRECTIONS: From Denver: Drive north on 28th Street; turn left (west) onto Lee Hill Road, which is right after the Holiday Drive-In sign. Take the first right into Tamberly Trade Center.

OTHER AMENITIES AT WINERY: Facilities available for private parties, weddings, rehearsal dinners, business meetings and non-profit fundraising events.

WINE AVAILABLE FOR PURCHASE OUTSIDE OF WINERY: Yes

OTHER TASTING ROOM LOCATIONS: No

NOTES: ______________________________

____

____

____

WILD CIDER

11455 CR 17, Firestone, CO 80504
303-532-9949
wildcider.com
adam@wildcider.com

OWNER: Adam Gorove

YEAR BEGAN OPERATION: 2013

AVERAGE CASES PRODUCED ANNUALLY: 30,000

WINES PRODUCED:
White: None
Red: None
Other: Cider: Agave Peach, Apple, Bee Hoppy, Berry, Pineapple, Pumpkin, Spiced Apple Pie

MESSAGE FROM OWNER: I went on a quest to find a well-balanced cider and nothing quenched my palette, so I created Wild Cider! Wild Cider has a very diverse portfolio of ciders. In 2014 our 1,100 tree orchard was planted on our 14 acre property. I look forward to seeing you all at our cidery as you sit back and enjoy the beautiful view of the Front Range Mountains. Cheers!

TASTING ROOM INFORMATION: Mid-May through October, Thursday through Saturday from 3 to 8 p.m.

DIRECTIONS: From I-25 and Exit #240: Head east on Firestone Blvd; turn left (north) onto CR 17; the cidery is on your left.

OTHER AMENITIES AT WINERY: Special event venue

WINE AVAILABLE FOR PURCHASE OUTSIDE OF WINERY: Yes

OTHER TASTING ROOM LOCATIONS: No

NOTES: ____

____

____

____

WILD WOMEN WINERY

1660 Champa Street, Denver, CO 80202
303-534-0788
winerydenver.com
winery@winerydenver.com

OWNER: Charlene and Ross Meriwether

YEAR BEGAN OPERATION: 2007

AVERAGE CASES PRODUCED ANNUALLY: 3,000

WINES PRODUCED:
White: Naked Chardonnay, Peach Chardonnay, Mandarin Orange Moscato, Pinot Grigio, Green Apple Riesling, Sauvignon Blanc
Reds: Barbera, Blackberry Merlot, Malbec, Petit Sirah, Pinot Noir, Pomegranate Zinfandel
Other: Several red blends; Grapefruit Blush; Chocolate Port

MESSAGE FROM OWNER: Wild Women Winery is a boutique winery that sources juice from California vineyards. Ross, the vintner, and his wife, Charlene, aka Chief Wild Woman, bring you 17 varietals ranging from a Naked Chardonnay to unusual blends such as the Hot Stiletto, a Zinfandel/Syrah blend. They include favorites such as Tempranillo and Barbera, and finish with their signature Royal Ruby, a chocolate port.

Each wine features its own entertaining label from the artwork of Annie Kier. Their compact winery operation and warm, inviting tasting room are found in the middle of downtown Denver, and offer tastings, wine by the glass, or wine by the bottle in a relaxing, fun atmosphere. Their motto: "If you're not having fun, we'll ask you to leave!"

TASTING ROOM INFORMATION: Tuesday through Sunday from noon to 8 p.m.

DIRECTIONS: From I-25 and Exit #210B (Auraria Parkway): Head northeast on Auraria Parkway; turn right (south) onto Speer Boulevard; turn left (northeast) onto Lawrence Street; turn right (south) onto 17th Street; turn right (southwest) onto Champa Street. Winery is on the left (north) side.

OTHER AMENITIES AT WINERY: Wine-related merchandise, personalized wine labels on any varietal, wine tasting parties, wine bottling parties

WINE AVAILABLE FOR PURCHASE OUTSIDE OF WINERY: Yes

OTHER TASTING ROOM LOCATIONS: No

NOTES: ____

____

____

____

FRONT RANGE REGION

What Else To See & Do

The area from Denver to Fort Collins, just east of the Rocky Mountains, is called the Front Range, and has something to offer everyone. Below is just a sampling of the 1,000+ things to see and do in this region. See individual cities and their websites for additional activities and information.

Arts and Museums **see city websites below**
From Picasso to Playwrights, there are hundreds of galleries, museums and performing centers along the Front Range. Here are just a few.

- **Clyfford Still Museum** **clyffordstillmuseum.org**
- **Denver Art Museum** **denverartmuseum.org**
- **Denver Center for the Performing Arts** **denvercenter.org**
- **Denver Museum of Nature and Science** **dmns.org**

Beer **mountainbrewbook.com**
Tired of wine? While that would be hard to believe, the Front Range offers tours and tastings at the big breweries - Anheuser-Busch, Miller-Coors, Odell and New Belgium, and at numerous micro-breweries.

Boulder **bouldercoloradousa.com**

Butterfly Pavilion **butterflies.org**
A tarantula walks on your hand? A butterfly lands on your head? Just some things to experience at this invertebrate and conservation center.

Colorado Renaissance Festival **coloradorenaissance.com**
Step back in time to 16th Century England at this summer festival featuring costumed merrymakers and artisans.

Colorado State Capitol **colorado.gov/capitoltour**
Find out where Colorado's laws are made and view the House and Senate galleries. You can tour the capitol building and learn about its history and construction.

Denver denver.org
Denver Botanic Gardens denverbotanicgardens.org
Get out your cameras or sketch pads and take a walk through the beautiful and innovative gardens that highlight plants from all over the world.

Denver Zoo denverzoo.org
Lions and tigers and bears, oh my! Enjoy this top attraction located on 80 acres in City Park, featuring over 4,000 animals.

Downtown Aquarium aquariumrestaurants.com
Swim little fishy, swim! That's what you will see at this entertainment and dining complex featuring 500+ species of aquatic life and other animals.

Elitch Gardens Theme Park elitchgardens.com
Dive, corkscrew, twist and turn at this 70-acre amusement park featuring thrill, family, kid and water rides.

Evergreen evergreenchamber.org
Estes Park visitestespark.com
Fort Collins visit.ftcollins.com

Gambling coloradocasinos.net
Is Lady Luck on your side? Find out at these casinos.

History historycolorado.org
Learn about when the West was wild and mining was predominant.

- **Buffalo Bill Museum and Grave** buffalobill.org
- **Byers-Evans House** historycolorado.org/museums
- **History Colorado Center** historycolorado.org/museums
- **Molly Brown House** mollybrown.org

Red Rocks Amphitheatre & Visitors Center redrocksonline.com
What bands played at Red Rocks in 1975? 1985? 2005? Find out at the Performer's Hall of Fame. In addition to their summer concert series, the Park offers hiking and biking trails and spectacular vistas.

Rocky Mountain National Park **nps.gov/romo**
From elk's bugling to hiking trails to the magnificent views on Trail Ridge Road, RMNP is truly nature's wonderland!

Sports
If you are thinking sports, the Front Range has them all:

- **Colorado Avalanche (hockey)** **avalanche.nhl.com**
- **Colorado Mammoth (lacrosse)** **coloradomammoth.com**
- **Colorado Rapids (soccer)** **coloradorapids.com**
- **Colorado Rockies (baseball)** **colorado.rockies.mlb.com**
- **Denver Broncos (football)** **denverbroncos.com**
- **Denver Nuggets (basketball)** **nba.com/nuggets**
- **Denver Outlaws (lacrosse)** **denveroutlaws.com**

U.S. Mint **usmint.gov/mint_tours**
Learn how to make money! Discover how your coins are made and what the little "D" stands for during your tour.

Pikes Peak Region

Wine Fact

Labels were first put on
wine bottles in the early 1700s,
but it wasn't until the 1860s
that suitable glues were developed
to hold them on the bottles.

http://www.beekmanwine.com/factsquotes.htm

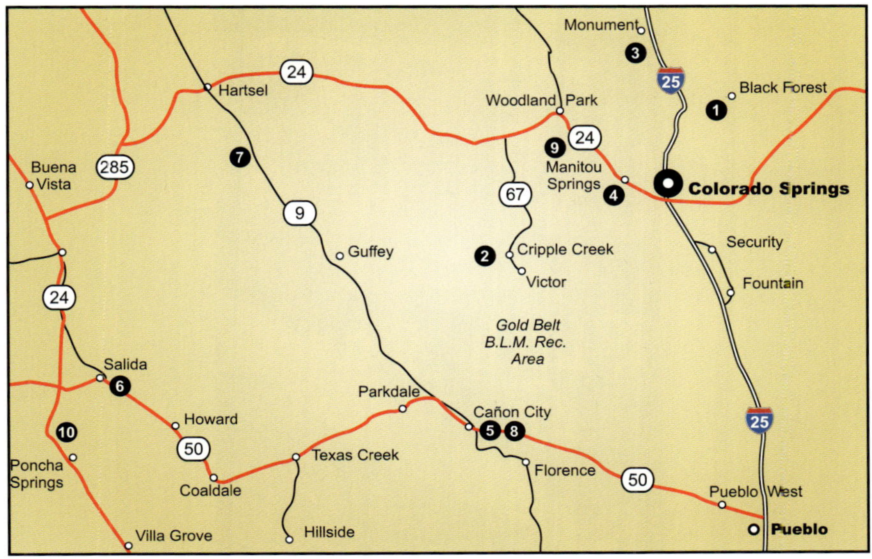

Pikes Peak Region Wineries

1. Black Forest Meadery
2. Byerscellars Wines
3. Catriona Cellars
4. D'Vine Wine - Manitou Springs
5. LeFuselier Winery @ Spring Creek Vineyards
6. Mountain Spirit Winery
7. Rockyspring Winery
8. The Winery at Holy Cross Abbey
9. The Winery at Pikes Peak
10. Vino Salida Wine Cellars

BLACK FOREST MEADERY

6420 Burrows Road, Unit A, Colorado Springs, CO 80908
719-495-7340
blackforestmeadery.com
mail@blackforestmeadery.com

OWNER: Adam and Shawna Shapiro

YEAR BEGAN OPERATION: 2007

AVERAGE CASES PRODUCED ANNUALLY: Information not Available

WINES PRODUCED:
White: None
Red: None
Other: Forest Mead, Mead in the Woods, Melody in the Woods and Wildfire; Mint and Lavender meads; Peach Melomel

MESSAGE FROM OWNER: The company was created in 2007 and is owned/operated by the Shapiro family. The sons (aka The Two Brothers) help in the planting of the vines, which were first started in pots. We thought, "Let's see what grows." We were surprised and impressed by the vines that can grow at 7,500' in Colorado. Typically, vines will grow 1.5' in the first growing year. Our vines grow around 5' in length, due to the soil and intense sunlight.

The vineyard is an experiment, and the experiment is a lesson in pride, delight, struggle and success. We have had good years and bad, but continue to research, test and gather results. Currently we are growing over 600 vines. Come visit our tasting room and delight in what we can produce!

TASTING ROOM INFORMATION: Memorial Day weekend to October, Thursday through Sunday from noon to 4 p.m.; other times by appointment only.

DIRECTIONS: From the intersection of I-25 at Exit #153, north of Colorado Springs: Exit at #153 onto Hwy 83 (Interquest Parkway); turn right (south) onto N. Powers Boulevard (Hwy 21); turn left (east) onto Old Ranch Road; turn left (north) onto Milam Road; turn right (east) onto Burgess Road; turn left (north) onto Burrows Road..

OTHER AMENITIES AT WINERY: T-shirts and trivets

WINE AVAILABLE FOR PURCHASE OUTSIDE OF WINERY: Yes

OTHER TASTING ROOM LOCATIONS: No

NOTES: ____

____

____

____

BYERSCELLARS WINES

Cripple Creek, CO 80813
303-570-5536
cripplecreekcellars.com
byerscellars@aol.com

OWNER: Nancy Byers

YEAR BEGAN OPERATION: 2010

AVERAGE CASES PRODUCED ANNUALLY: Information not Available

WINES PRODUCED:
White: Chardonnay
Red: Merlot
Other: Peach Chardonnay, Chocolate Cherry Merlot

MESSAGE FROM OWNER: High up in the Rocky Mountains there's a winery…Byerscellars Wines, LLC, which is a one-woman winery. It is located in the old western mining and gambling town of Cripple Creek, just west of Pikes Peak, at an elevation of 9,495'. We are dedicated to creating specialty wines in small batch production.

Byerscellars Wines makes some of the most unique and flavorful wines in Colorado. Our Peach Chardonnay is made with Palisade peaches and is a 100% Colorado product. What can we say about our Chocolate Cherry Merlot? It is a delicious combination of chocolate extract flavors and cherry, in the form of Montmorency Cherry juice, which has the perfect sweet/tart taste. One thing is for certain, the fantastic flavors will explode in your mouth. Make an appointment today to taste our delicious wines!

TASTING ROOM INFORMATION: By appointment only

DIRECTIONS: Provided at time of tasting appointment confirmation.

OTHER AMENITIES AT WINERY: N/A

WINE AVAILABLE FOR PURCHASE OUTSIDE OF WINERY: No

OTHER TASTING ROOM LOCATIONS: No

NOTES: ____

CARTRIONA CELLARS

243 Washington Street, Monument, CO 80132
719-481-3477
catrionacellars.com
catherine@catrionacellars.com

OWNER: Woody and Catherine Woodworth

YEAR BEGAN OPERATION: 2013

AVERAGE CASES PRODUCED ANNUALLY: 2,000

WINES PRODUCED:
White: Riesling, Sauvignon Blanc
Red: Cabernet Sauvignon, Zinfandel
Other: Various white and red blends; dry Rosé

MESSAGE FROM OWNER: Woody Woodworth has been making wine for 20 years. His passion led him and his wife Catherine (Catriona) to build a winery from an existing 1881 building. Two years of extensive remodel produced a state-of-the-art, sustainable winery with a tasting room, restaurant and courtyard patio on the grounds.

Chef prepared lunch and dinners accompany Catriona Cellars' award winning wines. Tours are available, but please call ahead for reservations. Please check our website for any restrictions.

TASTING ROOM INFORMATION: Tuesday through Saturday from 11:30 a.m. to 9 p.m.

DIRECTIONS: From I-25 and Exit #161: Head west to Washington Street; turn right (north) onto Washington Street; the winery is on your left.

OTHER AMENITIES AT WINERY: Open daily for lunch and dinner and additionally breakfast on Sundays; large venue for private parties with seating for 40 people inside and 50 in outside courtyard; special reservations available for intimate 8 guest dining.

WINE AVAILABLE FOR PURCHASE OUTSIDE OF WINERY: Yes

OTHER TASTING ROOM LOCATIONS: No

NOTES: ____

____

____

____

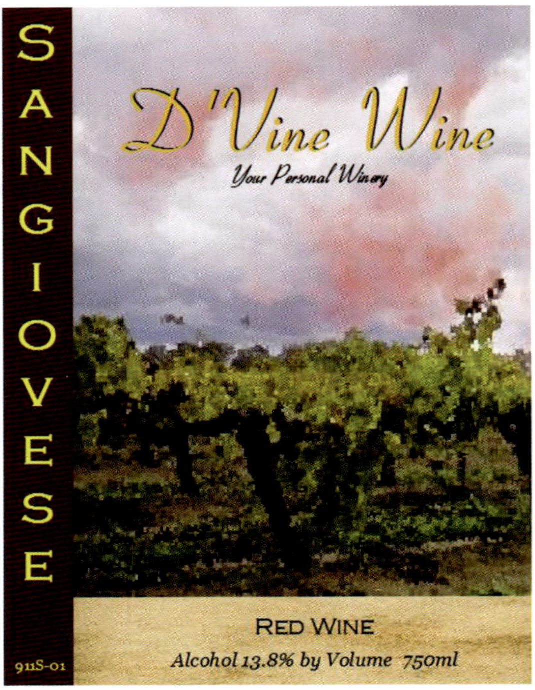

D'VINE WINE - MANITOU SPRINGS

934 Manitou Avenue #108, Manitou Springs, CO 80829
719-685-1030
winerymsprings.com
winery@winerymsprings.com

OWNER: Tracy Carole

YEAR BEGAN OPERATION: 2008

AVERAGE CASES PRODUCED ANNUALLY: 3,000

WINES PRODUCED:
White: Chardonnay, Pinot Grigio, Sauvignon Blanc
Red: Merlot, Pinot Noir, Sangiovese, Syrah
Other: Numerous red blends, Fruit wines, Port wines, Ice wine

MESSAGE FROM OWNER: D'Vine Wine-Manitou Springs is a boutique winery located in the historic spa building, in the heart of Manitou Springs. We import the highest quality grapes and then handcraft, blend and ferment all of our wines right in front of you! Drop in and enjoy a wine tasting, a glass of wine, or pick up a bottle.

Want to create a custom blend that is all your own? Our staff can guide you through making your very own wine! In addition to having a custom blend, you can enjoy a bottling party with friends, and each bottle will have your own personalized label.

TASTING ROOM INFORMATION: Monday through Saturday from noon to 8 p.m., Sunday from noon to 7 p.m.

DIRECTIONS: From the intersection of I-25 and Exit #141(Cimarron Street) in Colorado Springs: Head west towards Manitou Springs on Cimarron Street (Hwy 24); take the first exit on the right for Manitou Springs, which is just past 31st Street; winery is on the west end of historic downtown next to the Penny Arcade.

OTHER AMENITIES AT WINERY: Wine-related merchandise and light appetizers. We are available for private parties, events and weddings. Art work is available for purchase. We allow our customers to make their own wine and bottle it when it is ready.

WINE AVAILABLE FOR PURCHASE OUTSIDE OF WINERY: Yes

OTHER TASTING ROOM LOCATIONS: No

NOTES: ______________________________

____

____

____

LE FUSELIER WINERY @ SPRING CREEK VINEYARDS

1702 Willow Street, Cañon City, CO 81212
719-315-2075
site.coloradograpes.com
springcreekvineyards@hotmail.com

OWNER: David Fuselier

YEAR BEGAN OPERATION: 2009

AVERAGE CASES PRODUCED ANNUALLY: 500

WINES PRODUCED:
White: Pinot Grigio, Pinot Gris, Riesling
Red: Cabernet Sauvignon, Reserve Merlot
Other: Blends called Old World Blend, Cayuga White; Frontenac Nouveau, as well as many others

MESSAGE FROM OWNER: The Le Fuselier Winery at Spring Creek Vineyards is a small, family-operated village winery producing more than 30 different wines annually. David and Karin Fuselier make most of their wine from grapes they grow themselves or from 20 contract growers around town. Cañon City was settled by Italian immigrants, who brought grapes to grow in the city's remarkable, fruit-friendly climate, created by its position in a cul de sac cut into the Front Range of the Rockies. The Fuselier's hillside vineyard was hand-terraced to grow grapes more than 100 years ago and currently produces 13 different varieties.

TASTING ROOM INFORMATION: May, September through December, Saturday from noon to 5 p.m.

DIRECTIONS: From the intersection of Hwy 50 and Mackenzie Avenue on the east side of Cañon City: Head south on Mackenzie Avenue; turn right (northwest) onto Hwy 115. The winery is at the intersection of Hwy 115 and Willow Street.

OTHER AMENITIES AT WINERY: N/A

WINE AVAILABLE FOR PURCHASE OUTSIDE OF WINERY: No

OTHER TASTING ROOM LOCATIONS: No

NOTES: ______________________________

____

____

____

MOUNTAIN SPIRIT WINERY

15750 County Road 220, Salida, CO 81201
Mailing address: 16150 County Road 220, Salida, CO 81201
719-539-1175
mountainspiritwinery.com
barkett@mountainspiritwinery.com

OWNER: Terry and Michael Barkett

YEAR BEGAN OPERATION: 1995

AVERAGE CASES PRODUCED ANNUALLY: 2,500

WINES PRODUCED:
White: Chardonnay, Sophie's White, Symphony in White
Red: None
Other: Blends called Mountain Zin and Sophie's Red; Unique grape and fruit blends: Blackberry/Cabernet Franc, Blackberry/Chardonnay, Merlot/Raspberry, Angel Blush, Passion, dessert wines and Ice wine

MESSAGE FROM OWNER: Mountain Spirit Winery is a family-owned and operated boutique winery nestled in the high country of Colorado's Upper Arkansas Valley. Five acres of farmland, replete with apple orchards and an old homestead house, surrounded by 14,000' mountain vistas, establish the ambience for making Mountain Spirit premium wines. We have won over 50 national and international awards for our wines.

Co-winemakers Terry and Michael Barkett, bring educational backgrounds of clinical medicine, laboratory technology and computer science to the winemaker's art. The winemakers continue to push the limits of exploring new blends of wines, while maintaining the traditional, historic, high standards inherent to the gentle art of winemaking, giving rise to their motto: "Quality Wines, with a Difference."

TASTING ROOM INFORMATION: Summer, Daily from 10 a.m. to 5 p.m.; Winter, Monday through Saturday from 10 a.m. to 5 p.m.

DIRECTIONS: From the intersection of Hwy 285 and Hwy 50 north of Poncha Springs: Head west on Hwy 50; just before the town of Maysville, turn left (south) at the second County Road 220 turnoff; make an immediate left (east) onto County Road 220. The winery is just down the road.

OTHER AMENITIES AT WINERY: Picnic beneath 14,000' mountain peaks!

WINE AVAILABLE FOR PURCHASE OUTSIDE OF WINERY: No

OTHER TASTING ROOM LOCATIONS: Mountain Spirit Winery & Gallery, 8046 Hwy 50, Salida, CO 81201

NOTES: ____

____

____

____

ROCKYSPRING WINERY

1339 Wolfe Road, Hartsel, CO 80449
Winery: 720-324-2833, Denver area: 303-343-7454
rockyspringwinery.com
sales@rockyspringwinery.com

OWNER: Carlson Family

YEAR BEGAN OPERATION: 2009

AVERAGE CASES PRODUCED ANNUALLY: Information not Available

WINES PRODUCED:
White: Peach Apricot Chardonnay, Pinot Grigio, Green Apple Riesling, Riesling
Red: Cabernet Franc, Blackberry Cabernet, Pinot Noir, Sangiovese, Colorado Mountain Shiraz, Rockyspring Shiraz, Sweet Petite Sirah, Very Berry Shiraz, Red Zinfandel
Other: Blends called Muller Thurgau, Tropical Fruit Fuzion; White Zinfandel/Ice wine, Dessert wines and Port wines

MESSAGE FROM OWNER: Rockyspring Winery is a family-owned and operated winery/vineyard located in Park County, Colorado (South Park). We are dedicated to producing the highest quality, hand-crafted, artisan wines possible. All our wines are produced in limited quantities each year, based upon the quantity of grapes we are able to grow and the grapes we are able to obtain from other vineyards in Colorado. Each year increasing the number of vines in our vineyards, we look forward to all our wines being labeled "100% Colorado."

With the experience of four generations of winemakers, we feel you will find our wines to be a wonderful change from the everyday wines you may have experienced. Our production levels are intentionally small, but our quality is superb. We ask only that you try our wine, we truly believe you will like one or all of our superb wines.

TASTING ROOM INFORMATION: Thursday through Sunday from 10 a.m. to 5 p.m.

DIRECTIONS: From the intersection of Hwy 24 and Hwy 9 in Hartsel: Head south on Hwy 9, approximately 12 miles; turn right (west) onto Wolfe Road (MM35); continue 1.5 miles to winery. Wolfe Road is not an all-weather road, call ahead for conditions.

OTHER AMENITIES AT WINERY: A gift shop displaying local artisans' products for purchase. We are planning outdoor events in the future: concerts, grape picking and events for school groups.

WINE AVAILABLE FOR PURCHASE OUTSIDE OF WINERY: Yes

OTHER TASTING ROOM LOCATIONS: No

NOTES: ____

____

____

____

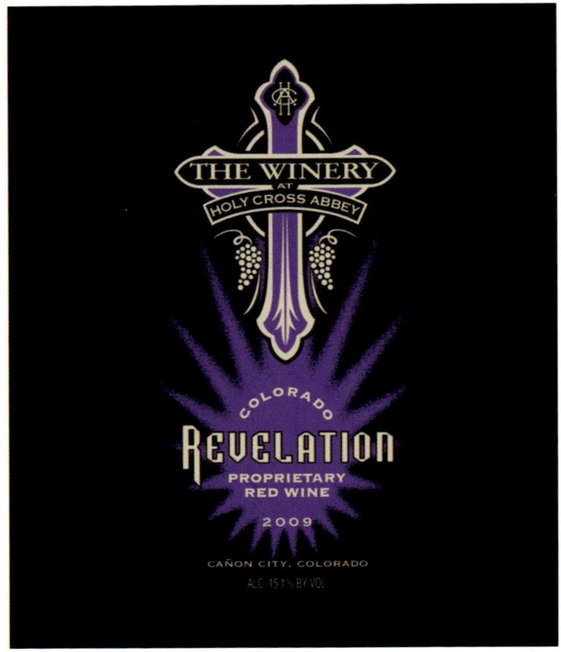

THE WINERY AT HOLY CROSS ABBEY

3011 E. Hwy 50, Cañon City, CO 81212
719-276-5191 or 877-422-9463 (HCA-WINE)
abbeywinery.com
sally@abbeywinery.com

OWNER: Larry and Diane Oddo and Sally Davidson

YEAR BEGAN OPERATION: 2001

AVERAGE CASES PRODUCED ANNUALLY: 14,000

WINES PRODUCED:
White: Chardonnay, Riesling, Sauvignon Blanc Reserve
Red: Cabernet Franc, Cabernet Sauvignon, Cabernet Sauvignon Reserve, Merlot, Merlot Reserve, Syrah
Other: Blends called Revelation, Sangre de Cristo Nouveau, Vineyard Sunset, Wild Cañon Harvest, Apple Blossom, Merlot Divinity

MESSAGE FROM OWNER: Eleven years ago some simple Benedictine Fathers had a dream. Today that dream is a reality! The Winery at Holy Cross Abbey was built by Sally Davidson and Matt Cookson in 2001, and it is now the largest and oldest winery in Cañon City, Colorado.

We carry 15 different wines, most of which are available year-round. All our wines are complimentary to sample in the tasting room, except the reserve wines, which are $1 each to taste.

Our wine selection caters to every taste, with an array from dry white, to dry red, to our sweeter series of wines. All of our wines have won numerous international awards.

TASTING ROOM INFORMATION: April through December, Monday through Saturday from 10 a.m. to 6 p.m., Sunday from noon to 5 p.m.; January through March, Monday through Saturday from 10 a.m. to 5 p.m., Sunday from noon to 5 p.m.

DIRECTIONS: From the intersection of Hwy 50 and Mackenzie Avenue in eastern Cañon City: Head west on Hwy 50. The Winery is located just west of Dozier Avenue.

OTHER AMENITIES AT WINERY: Park facilities

WINE AVAILABLE FOR PURCHASE OUTSIDE OF WINERY: Yes

OTHER TASTING ROOM LOCATIONS: No

NOTES: ______________________________

____

____

____

THE WINERY AT PIKES PEAK

4455 Fountain Avenue, Cascade, CO 80809
719-684-8000
wineryatpikespeak.com
thewineryatpikespeak@live.com

OWNER: Marvin Parliament

YEAR BEGAN OPERATION: 2013

AVERAGE CASES PRODUCED ANNUALLY: 1,500

WINES PRODUCED:
White: Chardonnay, Pinot Gris, Riesling
Red: Cabernet Sauvignon
Other: Parliament Blend, Rosie C

MESSAGE FROM OWNER: In an attempt to better accommodate our neighborhood and to provide a venue for hosting an event or out of town guests, the Parliaments expanded around the corner from their Wines of Colorado facility and created The Winery at Pikes Peak. Our new winery is located in an historic, 8,000 sq. ft. building, which at one time housed automobiles that were used for touring to the top of Pikes Peak.

The Winery provides complimentary wine tasting of our 6 signature wines. The Parliament Blend, named after the proprietors, is a unique blend of Cabernet and Syrah, and our Rosie C is named after the matriarch of the family, Rosie Chamandy.

At our Wines of Colorado location we are proud to offer the largest selection of Colorado wines in the state. Here you can enjoy shopping in our retail wine store and gift shop or enjoy a unique dining experience in the shade of the willows and pines next to Fountain Creek. Whether you are at The Winery at Pikes Peak or at Wines of Colorado you can enjoy the Colorado experience you have been looking for.

TASTING ROOM INFORMATION: Wednesday through Sunday from 9 a.m. to 7 p.m.

DIRECTIONS: From Colorado Springs: Head west on Hwy 24 for 10 miles to the town of Cascade. Turn left (south) onto Fountain Avenue. The winery is on the right side of the road.

OTHER AMENITIES AT WINERY: A restaurant serving appetizers; a facility for private parties

WINE AVAILABLE FOR PURCHASE OUTSIDE OF WINERY: Yes

OTHER TASTING ROOM LOCATIONS: Wines of Colorado, 8045 W. Hwy 24, Cascade, CO 80809

NOTES: ____

____

____

____

____

VINO SALIDA WINE CELLARS

8100 W. Hwy 50, Unit B, Salida, CO 81201
10495 W. CR120, Ponha Springs, CO 81242
Mailing address: PO Box 43, Salida, CO 81201
719-539-6299
vinosalida.com
steve@vinosalida.com

OWNER: Steve Flynn

YEAR BEGAN OPERATION: 2009

AVERAGE CASES PRODUCED ANNUALLY: 1,500

WINES PRODUCED:
White: Riesling, Viognier
Red: Merlot, Petite Sirah, Syrah
Other: Blends called Vino Bianco di Salida, Vino Rosso di Salida, Vino Rosato di Salida, Vino Novello di Salida; Bee Vino, a honey mead.

MESSAGE FROM OWNER: Opened in 2009 in Salida, Colorado, Vino Salida Wine Cellars is a small, artisan winery in the heart of the Colorado Rocky Mountains. Steve Flynn, winemaker/owner, caught the "wine bug" in 2002 when he experienced his first grape crush while working for Mountain Spirit Winery. He works closely with grape growers in Palisade and Paonia, a local honey producer and a small cooperage in Kentucky to produce unique varietals and tasty blends.

At harvest, Steve's goal is to express the grower's art by encouraging a slow and natural fermentation, slowly allowing the wines to showcase their own personality in the glass. The result is a true reflection of Colorado terroir that pairs well with local foods. The wines are inviting to the palate, full of character, flavor and body that linger from start to finish, leaving you with a desire to taste more! When you enter the Vino Salida Tasting Parlour, you are welcomed by friendly staff and will be offered wine tasting and a casual winery tour.

TASTING ROOM INFORMATION: Monday through Saturday from 10 a.m. to 6 p.m., Sunday from noon to 5 p.m.

DIRECTIONS: From the intersection of Hwy 50 and Holman Avenue in Salida: Head west on Hwy 50. The winery is on the north side just past Wal-Mart. For new winery location as of 9/1/15 – From Hwy 285 and Hwy 50: Head south; turn left (east) onto CR 120; the winery is on your right.

OTHER AMENITIES AT WINERY: Custom wine tasting events for up to 20 people in the Barrel Room.

WINE AVAILABLE FOR PURCHASE OUTSIDE OF WINERY: Yes

OTHER TASTING ROOM LOCATIONS: Wanderlust Road, 146 W. 1st Street, Salida, CO 81201

NOTES: ____________________

____

____

____

PIKES PEAK REGION

What Else To See & Do

Cave of the Winds **caveofthewinds.com**
Head underground into a mile of caverns that were discovered in 1881. Three educational tours of varying lengths and difficulty help you explore these cave formations by flashlight or hand-held lanterns.

Cheyenne Mountain Zoo **cmzoo.org**
Give an 18" long giraffe tongue a cookie? You can at this zoo, which combines breathtaking scenery with more than 700 animals. Your admission ticket includes the spectacular drive to the Will Rogers Shrine built in the 1930s.

Colorado Springs Sky Sox **skysox.com**
"Take me out to the ball game." The Colorado Springs Sky Sox are the AAA affiliate of the Milwaukee Brewers. Day or night games are available.

Florissant Fossil Beds National Monument **nps.gov/flfo**
Stretch your legs and take a short, self-guided walk around this exciting fossil deposit. The park and Visitor Center display fossil deposits, massive petrified redwood trees and fossils of insects and leaves.

Gambling **visitcripplecreek.com**
Try your luck and seek your fortune at one of the many casinos in Cripple Creek. You can also travel back in time to the Gold Rush days in this historic town, which offers breathtaking views, mine tours and shopping.

Garden of the Gods Visitor & Nature Center **gardenofgods.com**
"How Did Those Red Rocks Get There?" Watch the movie at the Visitor Center and find out, then explore the magnificent 300' towering sandstone rock formations. Pikes Peak is the backdrop to this national landmark.

Outdoor Activities

- **Hiking, Biking and '14ers** **trails.com & numerous websites**
  There are hundreds of trails in the Pikes Peak region. Interested in climbing a 14,000' mountain? Chaffee County is home to 15!

- **Rafting** **canoncitycolorado.com**
  Sense the adrenaline rush as you paddle down the Arkansas River! This website provides a list of companies offering rafting trips and adventures.

Pikes Peak **pikespeak.us.com**
Test your brakes, grip the wheel and then drive the 19-mile Pikes Peak Highway to the 14,115' summit. On a clear day, the 360-degree panorama offers views of Colorado Springs, the eastern plains and the Continental Divide. It was "discovered" by Lt. Zebulon Pike in 1806, and Katharine Lee Bates was inspired to write "America the Beautiful" from its summit.

Pikes Peak Cog Railway **cograilway.com**
If you would rather leave the driving to someone else, the cog railroad is your answer! Since 1891, the Railway has transported millions of people along the 9-mile track to the summit of Pikes Peak. Reservations a must!

ProRodeo Hall of Fame **prorodeohalloffame.com**
Put on your cowboy/girl boots and visit the only heritage center in the world devoted to professional rodeo. After viewing a history film, visitors can explore the museum that pays tribute to the American cowboy.

Royal Gorge Bridge **royalgorgebridge.com**
Are you acrophobic? Then the view from the 956' suspension bridge might be difficult! Although the June 2013 wildfire destroyed most of the area, the park and Visitors Center are rebuilding, and the bridge still stands!

Royal Gorge Train **royalgorgeroute.com**
"All aboard"...take a ride on the rails behind a 1950s streamliner taking in the scenery of the Royal Gorge and Arkansas River. The train offers several unique options: breakfast, lunch or even a dinner with wine experience, a mystery train and, in December, ride the Polar Express Train.

United States Air Force Academy **usafa.af.mil/information/visitors**
Experience the core values of Integrity First, Service Before Self and Excellence In All We Do at the USAF Academy. Visitors may access several areas including the spectacular Cadet Chapel, Falcon Stadium and the Visitor Center.

For further information, please visit these websites:

canoncity.com
canoncitycolorado.com
manitousprings.org
nowthisiscolorado.com
salidachamber.org
salida.com
visitcripplecreek.com
visitcos.com

Mountains Region

Wine Fact

When Tutankhamen's tomb was opened in 1922, the wine jars buried with him were labeled with the year, the name of the winemaker, and comments such as "very good wine." The labels were so specific that they could actually meet modern wine label laws of several countries.

http://facts.randomhistory.com/2009/08/21_wine.html

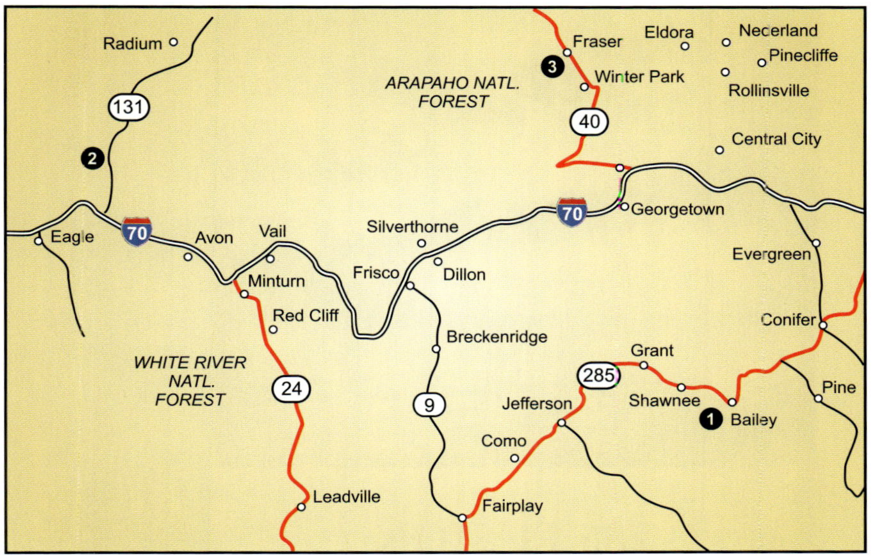

Mountains Region Wineries

1. Aspen Peak Cellars
2. Vines at Vail Winery
3. Winter Park Winery

ASPEN PEAK CELLARS

60750 US Hwy 285, Bailey, CO 80421
303-816-5504
aspenpeakcellars.com
info@aspenpeakcellars.com

OWNER: Marcel and Julie Flukiger

YEAR BEGAN OPERATION: 2009

AVERAGE CASES PRODUCED ANNUALLY: 1,700

WINES PRODUCED:
White: Pinot Grigio, Riesling, Sauvignon Blanc
Red: Barbera, Cabernet Sauvignon, Pinot Noir, Zinfandel
Other: Blends called 285 Fusion and Conifer Red; Strawberry Rosé; Pomegranate Rouge; Blanc de Blancs (sparkling wine); Mocha Zinsation

MESSAGE FROM OWNER: Marcel and Julie Flukiger developed a passion for winemaking several years ago, when Marcel bought Julie a winemaking kit for Christmas. The hobby got out of control, and in 2009 they started commercial production at the historic Clifton House Inn in Conifer. Unfortunately in the summer of 2011 lightning struck the 140-year old barn on the property, resulting in the loss of their special events venue. This led to moving their business to a new, larger winemaking facility in Bailey, which opened in 2012.

Aspen Peak Cellars produces about 1,700 cases of wine annually from grapes grown in the most consistent wine regions in the country. In addition to winemaking the Flukigers offer a variety of events at the winery. Every Saturday from 2 to 5 p.m. live entertainment from many of the talented, local musicians is provided. Along with your wine you can enjoy a wide selection of artisan meats and cheeses, which are available for purchase, to create your own antipasto. The Wine Club is the perfect way to learn more about Aspen Peaks' fun establishment, which includes a quarterly, private party event with a 3-course buffet dinner and a glass of wine.

TASTING ROOM INFORMATION: Wednesday through Sunday from 11 a.m. to 5 p.m.

DIRECTIONS: From the intersection of Hwy 285 and C-470: Head south on Hwy 285 to downtown Bailey; turn left (south) off the highway to the winery.

OTHER AMENITIES AT WINERY: Various events - Live Music every Saturday from 2 to 5 p.m., wine dinners, snowshoe and fondue events; Gift shop; Shaded patio, picnic tables by the river and picnic foods available; the winery is available to rent for private party event; winery tours.

WINE AVAILABLE FOR PURCHASE OUTSIDE OF WINERY: Yes

OTHER TASTING ROOM LOCATIONS: Grow Your Own, 27051 Barkley Road, Conifer, CO 80433

NOTES: ____

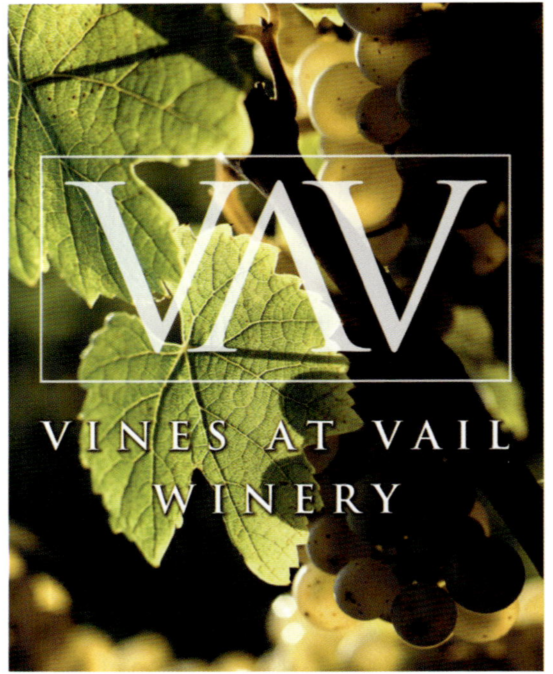

VINES AT VAIL WINERY

4 Eagle Ranch, 4098 Hwy 131, Wolcott, CO 81655
Mailing address: PO Box 18296, Avon, CO 81620
970-949-9463
vinesatvailwinery.com
info@vinesatvailwinery.com

OWNER: Patrick Chirichillo

YEAR BEGAN OPERATION: 2012

AVERAGE CASES PRODUCED ANNUALLY: 2,000

WINES PRODUCED:
White: Moscato, Pinot Grigio
Red: Barbera, Cabernet Sauvignon, Grenache, Malbec, Petite Syrah, Primitivo, Ruby Cabernet, Syrah
Other: Blends called: Three Way, Cotes du Vail, Davos, New House of Papi, Prima, Super Tuscan Style, Vail Bella, Vail Ink; Grenache Rosé

MESSAGE FROM OWNER: Like the wines we craft, we are a character-driven, modest mountain winery specializing in handcrafted, small lot wines from grapes sourced in California, that honor our winemaking heritage.

Vail Valley resident and real estate broker for more than 25 years, Patrick Chirichillo was raised in a long line of family winemakers. He became interested in the winemaking process at the age of nine—helping his grandfather in a traditional home production. During this time, he learned more than how to cultivate a distinct wine; he discovered a deep-seeded passion for a creative process that promotes storytelling and sharing life's moments with friends and family.

Spanning the past 10 years, Patrick's wines have garnered numerous annual awards from the Colorado Mountain Winefest Amateur Winemakers Competition. And in 2014, Vines at Vail officially became a commercial winery. We look forward to expanding our reach and winning more awards as we embark on a new phase in our winemaking journey.

TASTING ROOM INFORMATION: Memorial Day through Labor Day, open daily from noon to 6 p.m. Other times by appointment only.

DIRECTIONS: From I-70 at Exit #157 (Wolcott/Steamboat Springs): Turn right (north) off exit ramp; turn left (west) onto Hwy 6; turn right (north) onto Hwy 131. Continue on Hwy 131 for 4 miles to 4 Eagle Ranch, located on the right.

OTHER AMENITIES AT WINERY: Facility available for all event functions and has a restaurant onsite. During the summer, horseback riding, cattle round-ups, zip line tours, rafting, rock climbing, Jeep and ATV tours and a petting zoo are available. During the winter months enjoy snowmobiling, dogsled adventures and sleigh rides.

WINE AVAILABLE FOR PURCHASE OUTSIDE OF WINERY: Yes

OTHER TASTING ROOM LOCATIONS: No

NOTES: ______________________________

____

____

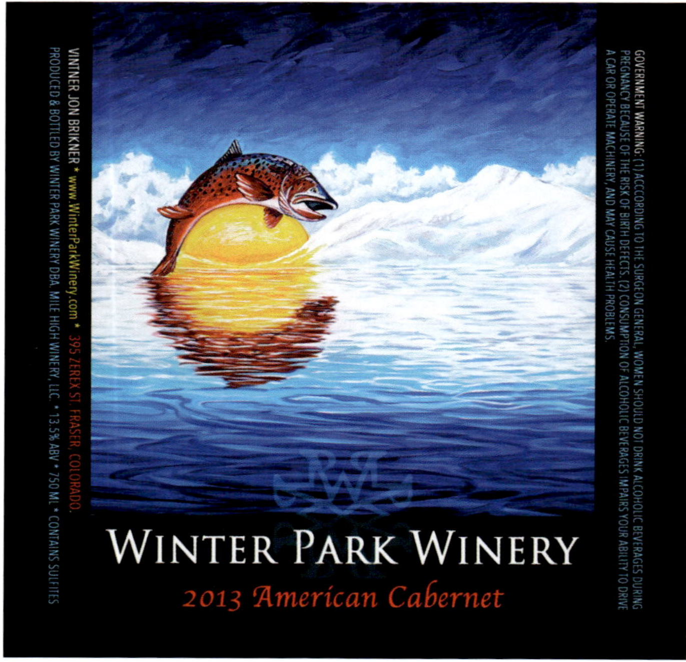

WINTER PARK WINERY

395 Zerex Street, Fraser, CO 80442
970-726-4514
winterparkwinery.com
jon@winterparkwinery.com

OWNER: Jon Brickner

YEAR BEGAN OPERATION: 2004

AVERAGE CASES PRODUCED ANNUALLY: 1,000

WINES PRODUCED:
White: Chardonnay, Riesling, White Zinfandel
Red: Cabernet Sauvignon, Merlot, Syrah
Other: Blend called Grateful Red; Port wine

MESSAGE FROM OWNER: Located in downtown Fraser along US Hwy 40, the Winter Park Winery prides itself on its wine, small town charm and great atmosphere. Like the wine, it offers a bold, rich and flavorful spice to the local community, and invites locals and visitors alike to come and experience the festivities. All of our wines are made onsite and are handcrafted to achieve the best quality red and white wines. All of our wine is unfiltered to maintain full-mouth feel and flavor, while keeping all of the nutrients wine has to offer.

In addition to our wines, we also have the Winter Park Winery Bike Team, which competes in sport, expert and pro categories. Be sure to check our website frequently or sign-up for our "ezine" to hear about specials, music and events happening at the winery!

TASTING ROOM INFORMATION: Daily, from 12:30 to 6 p.m.; May and November by appointment.

DIRECTIONS: Located in downtown Fraser, which is just north of Winter Park, on Hwy 40 (Zerex Street).

OTHER AMENITIES AT WINERY: N/A

WINE AVAILABLE FOR PURCHASE OUTSIDE OF WINERY: No

OTHER TASTING ROOM LOCATIONS: No

NOTES: ______________________________

____

____

____

____

____

MOUNTAINS REGION

What Else To See & Do

The Mountains Region covers a vast amount of area with numerous things to see and do in the cities and counties that encompass the central Rockies. Below is a small sampling of activities and locations. See the Internet for further information.

Aspen **aspenchamber.org**

Georgetown **georgetown-colorado.org**

Georgetown Train **georgetownlooprr.com**
Let the journey begin as you travel from Silver Plume down 600' to Georgetown and back. When completed in 1884, the route was considered an engineering marvel. Reservations highly recommended.

Ghost Towns **ghosttowns.com/states/co/co.html**
How did the town become established? Who lived there? Why did they leave? Colorado is teeming with ghost towns packed with western history.

Glenwood Springs **visitglenwood.com**

Grand County **visitgrandcounty.com**

Hot Springs **colorado.com/activities/hot-springs**
Need to soak and relax after all your wine tasting? Try one of Colorado's 27 hot springs located throughout the state. Colorado.com has the entire list, so check out the website before you travel into any Wine Region. Here are just a few:

- **Cottonwood Hot Spring & Inn** **cottonwood-hot-springs.com**
- **Glenwood Hot Springs** **hotspringspool.com**
- **Mt Princeton Hot Springs Resort** **mtprinceton.com**
- **Strawberry Park Hot Springs** **strawberryhotsprings.com**
- **The Springs Resort & Spa** **pagosahotsprings.com**

Leadville **leadville.com**

Maroon Bells **aspenchamber.org**

The Maroon Bells are considered to be the most photographed peaks in Colorado. Any season of the year provides breathtaking scenery.

Mine tours **colorado.com/colorado-mine-tours**

"Is there any more gold in them thar hills?" Learn about Colorado's mining history and see where prospectors spent their time. There are a variety of mine tours throughout the Mountain Region. Here are just a few:

- **Breckenridge** **countryboymine.com**
- **Idaho Springs** **phoenixmine.com**
- **Silverton** **minetour.com**

Mount Evans **mountevans.com**

Ever been to the top of North America's highest paved auto road? Drive to the top of Mount Evans (elevation 14,264') for the experience of a lifetime, as you pass through several ecosystems and glimpse the state animal (Rocky Mountain Bighorn Sheep).

Outdoor Activities

Winter, Spring, Summer or Fall the Rocky Mountains have it all! Whatever your interests or abilities, the Mountain Region provides incredible outdoor enjoyment.

- **Cross-Country Skiing and Snowshoeing** **trails.com / individual city & county websites**
- **Fishing** **coloradofishing.net**
- **Hiking and Biking** **14ers.com / trails.com / individual city & county websites**
- **Rafting** **colorado.com/activities/colorado-rafting**
- **Skiing / Boarding (downhill)** **coloradoski.com**

Park County **parkco.us**

Redstone Castle **redstonecastle.us**

There is a castle in Colorado? Yes, built in 1897 for coal and steel magnate John Cleveland Osgood.

Summit County summitchamber.org
- **Breckenridge** gobreck.com
- **Copper Mountain** coppercolorado.com
- **Dillon** townofdillon.com
- **Frisco** townoffrisco.com
- **Keystone** keystone.travel
- **Silverthorne** silverthorne.org

Winter Park winterparkgov.com

Vail vail.com

REFERENCES

Colorado Wine Industry Board. *Colorado: a Beautiful State of Wine.* 2011. Print.

Fay, Abbott. *The Story of Colorado Wines*. First. Montrose, CO: Western Reflections Publishing Company, 2002.

"FoodAndWinePairing." Food and Wine Pairing. Unknown, 2012. Web. 10 Apr. 2015

Hawkins, Anthony. "Glossary of Wine Tasting Terminology." 1.4. (1995): n.pag. Web. November, 2011. http://zebra.sc.edu/smell/wine_glossary.html.

Marshall, Wes. *What's A Wine Lover To Do?*. First. New York, NY: Artisan, a division of Workman Publishing Company, Inc., 2010.

McCarthy, Ed, Mary Ewing-Mulligan, and Maryann Egan. *Wine All-In-One For Dummies.* First. Hoboken, NJ: Wiley Publishing, Inc., 2009.

Smith, Alta and Brad. *The Guide to Colorado Wineries.* Second. Golden, CO: Fulcrum Publishing, 2002.

Walton, Stuart. *Cook's Encyclopedia of Wine.* First. New York, NY: Barnes & Noble, Inc., 2005

Wikipedia. November 2012. http://en.wikipedia.or.

"Wine Facts." *Beekman Wines & Liquors* (1996): n.pag. Web. 3 Feb 2012. http://www.beekmanwine.com/factsquotes.htm.

"Wine Grapes." *Keep Wine Simple* (2008): n.pag. Web. November 2012. http://www.keepwinesimple.com/index.html.

Zraly, Kevin. *Windows On The World / Complete Wine Course.* First. New York, NY: Sterling Publishing, 2009.

LOCAL REFERENCES

Colorado Wine Industry Board

In 1977 the Colorado General Assembly enacted the Colorado Limited Winery Act to permit small "farm wineries", which paved the way for more commercial wineries to open. By 1990, the industry had developed to the extent that the General Assembly passed the Colorado Wine Industry Development Act. This created the Colorado Wine Industry Development Board, under the authority of the Colorado Department of Agriculture.

The CWIDB is comprised of nine members, who represent a variety of wine-industry fields. They are appointed by the Governor and the position is voluntary. In general, the board oversees the excise tax revenues and the $0.01/liter tax from Colorado wineries. These funds are used for research and development (overseen by Colorado State University) and for the marketing and promotion of Colorado wines and grapes. For more information: *www.ColoradoWine.com*

Colorado Association for Viticulture and Enology

The Colorado Association for Viticulture and Enology (CAVE) is an association that exists to encourage and support enology and viticulture in Colorado. CAVE promotes the interests of Colorado grape growers and wineries in legislative and political matters, provides a forum for the exchange of ideas and to disseminate current information pertaining to optimum winemaking and agriculture practices for vineyards in the area. CAVE seeks to establish contacts and relationships with other associations, both regional and statewide, to further development and growth of the industry.

Colorado Mountain Winefest and Colorado Urban Winefest are the fundraisers for CAVE, and all funds go toward education, seminars, research and equipment purchases to improve the grape growing and winemaking of Colorado wines. For more information: *www.winecolorado.org*.

Colorado Viticulture Information and Data

Through the Colorado Agricultural Experiment Station (AES) and Colorado State University, you can find statistics on Colorado's grape growing activities and other viticulture practices.

The Western Colorado Research Center is part of the AES network and is located south of Grand Junction. Its vision is to meet emerging and recognized needs of the western Colorado agricultural community and attempt to overcome challenges, solve problems, and create opportunities within the region and beyond.

For additional information, visit their website: *www.aes-wcrc.agsci.colostate.edu/*

Colorado Proud

Colorado Proud is a program of the Colorado Department of Agriculture, promotes food and agricultural products that are grown, raised or processed in Colorado.

Visit *www.ColoradoProud.org* to learn more.

INDEX

ACKNOWLEDGMENTS

I would first like to thank my husband, Jim. It was his information about a Colorado microbrewery guidebook that inspired me to create the first edition of *Exploring Colorado Wineries*. Thanks, Jim, for the constant support and guidance you have given me.

Thanks are extended to all the people who purchased the first edition. It has been incredible to see the enthusiasm for learning about Colorado's wine industry! I would also like to extend my appreciation to all the people and companies who helped promote the book.

My deepest gratitude is extended to Nick Zelinger of NZ Graphics, who again made this book come to life. His creativity and expertise made this guidebook a thing of beauty. I also want to thank him for putting my work ahead of others and completing the project quickly.

I am grateful to my daughter, Allison, who used her editing skills from her publishing internship to help me with this book.

A special thank you is given to Debra Ray, owner of Desert Moon Vineyards, who provided the picture of the Book Cliff Mountains for the front cover, Jacob Helleckson of Stone Cottage Cellars, who provided the picture of the West Elk Mountains for the back cover and to Jim Cox, of JC Photography in Palisade, for the Grand Valley Region picture.

Thank you all for your assistance!

ABOUT THE AUTHOR

Paula Mitchell has combined her interest in wine and passion for Colorado into this guidebook. Before writing the first edition of *Exploring Colorado Wineries*, she wanted to learn more about her own state's wine industry. Since then she has traveled all around Colorado, conducted "wine exploring" presentations, attended numerous wine festivals and earned her Level 2 Sommelier certification...and along the way enjoyed some delicious Colorado wines!

The purpose of her guidebook is to help others explore and discover Colorado's wineries, so they too can experience and savor Colorado wines.

Paula lives in the metro Denver area with her husband and two daughters. This is her second guidebook.

For more information, to purchase the book or to schedule a presentation, please contact the author through her website at *www.ExploringColoradoWineries.com.*

NOTES:

NOTES:

NOTES:

NOTES:

NOTES: